THE
GARDEN
PROBLEM
SOLVER

Published exclusively for Asda Stores Limited,
Southbank, Great Wilson Street, Leeds LS11 5AD
by Quarto Concept
6 Blundell Street, London N7 9BH

ISBN 1 85348 087 8

Creative Director — Michael Tout
Joint Editorial Managers — Debbie Clarke, Belinda Giles
Planning Manager — Barry Kelly
Design — Karen Byrne, Fiona Russell, Edwin Tingey
Illustrator — Richard Irving
Jacket Design — Lee Robinson

Printed in Hong Kong by
Leefung-Asco Printers Limited

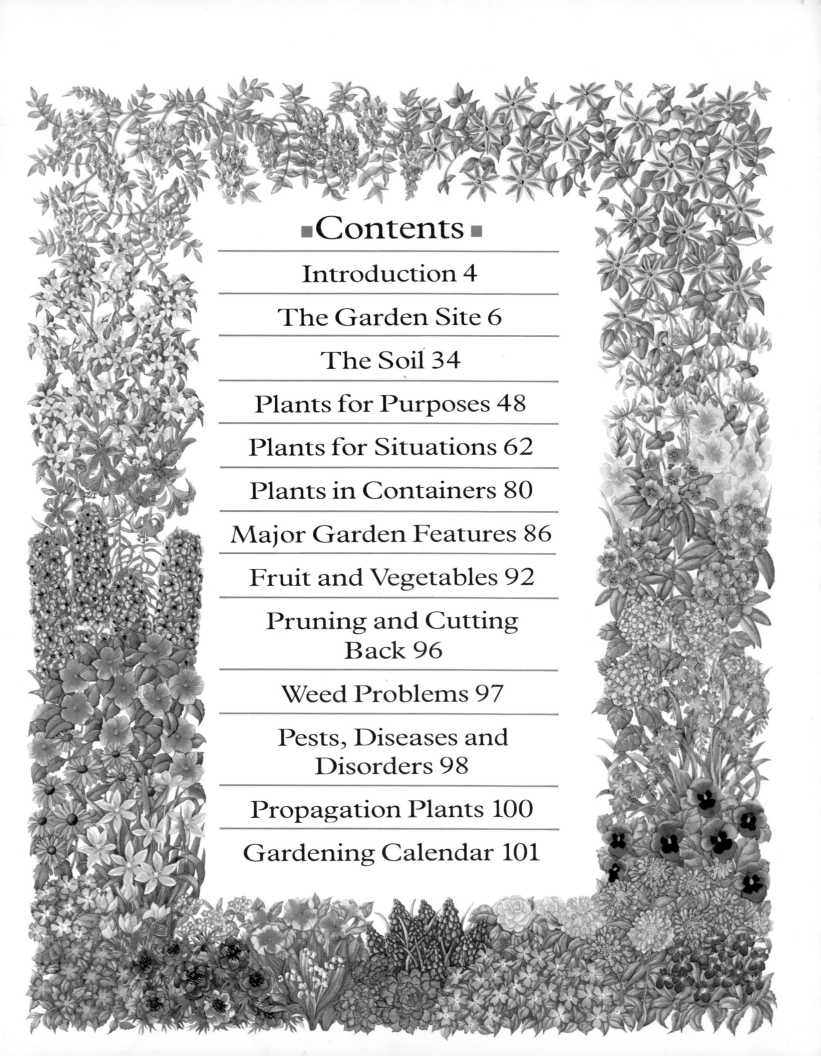

∎Contents∎

INTRODUCTION

Prevention is always better than cure, and that applies in gardening as much as anywhere else. A little extra care and thought early on will so often save a great deal of trouble and worry later.

It is vital to study your garden closely; its situation and environs, its soil and climate; before laying plans, so that potential problems may be spotted in advance and either be overcome or allowed for in your schemes. Aim to avoid making those basic mistakes which will cause constant irritation in years to come; mistakes like choosing the wrong plant, shrub or tree for the situation, planting without proper soil preparation, pruning at the wrong time of year, and so on.

When choosing your plants, always try to find out as much as possible about them before buying and planting. Check in gardening reference books and encyclopaedias to discover — in detail — exactly what you can expect from the plants, as well as what they, in return, must have if they are to give of their best. Remember that the greater care you take in meeting the individual requirements of your plants and in improving and maintaining the condition of your soil, the fewer problems you are likely to face in later years. Well-grown plants, given the conditions they most enjoy, planted in well-prepared soil, correctly fed and watered, and regularly supplied with garden compost or other humus materials, are far less likely to succumb to pests and diseases than plants struggling in poor conditions or unsuitable situations.

THE GARDEN SITE

Are there basic problems with your garden site which need to be identified and either corrected or allowed for in your gardening plans? Most gardens — especially brand new ones — suffer from at least one or two basic disadvantages which make successful gardening difficult or awkward in one way or another. Your worries may be major, such as severe extremes of climate, lack of wind shelter; difficult soil-type; or they may be niggling troubles, like excessive shade, overgrown or weed-infested areas, steep slopes, ugly views or a boring garden layout. The earlier these elementary problems are pinpointed and either tackled or allowed for, the easier you will make life for yourself later on.

How do location and local

climate affect the garden?

WINTER COLD

Most obviously, the further north your garden, the shorter and cooler the summers, and the harsher the winter conditions are likely to be. Various sun-loving, tender or semi-hardy shrubs and perennial border plants (and even some supposedly hardy shrubs and plants) which thrive and are long-lived in warm southern counties tend not to do so well in colder northern gardens. They may need to be planted against a warm, sunny wall and be given other winter protection; or they may not survive at all, despite your attempts at providing winter shelter.

Autumn planting and soil-cultivation will also usually have to be carried out earlier in the north than in the south (since autumn rains and winter frosts arrive sooner in northern regions). Similarly, in northern gardens where winter lingers longer than in the south, spring planting, sowing and soil-working will quite likely have to be delayed until somewhat later than is normally recommended.

Inland gardens far from the nearest coast also tend to be much colder in winter than those close to the sea.

Slightly tender plants and shrubs usually, therefore, stand a better chance of surviving winter in a coastal garden than in an inland garden at the same latitude. This is most noticeable on the south-west and west coasts of Great Britain (swept by the warm, oceanic Gulf Stream), but it also applies, to a lesser degree, to all other coastal areas.

Gardens on high ground are generally colder than those closer to sea-level — a drop of about 1°F (0.6°C) in average temperatures throughout the year for every 300ft (100m) above sea level — and north-facing or north-east-facing slopes are always colder (and shadier) than those facing south or south-west.

On the other hand, a low lying garden which sits in a 'frost pocket' – a valley or other hollow,

or a dip where cold air flows down and collects from surrounding higher ground — can be exceptionally cold in winter; often much colder than gardens on the surrounding high ground. A small-scale frost pocket may also occur within a garden on a sloping site where a barrier, such as a wall, a solid fence or a dense hedge, blocks the flow of cold air running down from higher ground above. Here a localized pocket of freezing air may gather in winter, scorching plants and shrubs.

Gardens in the heart of a city or large town, surrounded by masses of heat-storing concrete, bricks and tarmac, will always be slightly warmer than gardens further out in the countryside, and are therefore a slightly safer bet for less hardy plants.

WIND EXPOSURE

Sites on high ground and steep slopes are always particularly windy, and so too are gardens in coastal areas, where winter gales blowing in from far out at sea can cause severe damage. For gardens near coasts, there is the additional and often serious problem of salt spray, which can easily be carried for miles inland on high winds, damaging plant growth and doubling the stunting effects of blustery weather.

RAINFALL

The wettest areas in Great Britain are the west and the north (particularly on high ground); conditions become gradually drier towards the east. Driest of all is the south-east of England — roughly east of a line drawn from the River Humber to the Isle of Wight — where summer droughts tend to be the most severe.

How can you beat the weather?

Bearing the above points in mind, you should carefully study your garden's position and its surroundings and take these into account in your plans. Generally, the best policy is to flow with the stream and adapt your planting schemes as much as possible to the local climate (with perhaps the occasional more adventurous and risky choice). Local nurserymen should know from experience which plants are likely to do well in your area and which are likely to fail, and this should be reflected in the basic range of plants they offer. Their advice is well worth seeking and listening to — along with the advice of other private gardeners in your area.

Where severe winter cold seems likely to be a serious problem, or where experience has shown it to be a worry — supposedly permanent plants and shrubs repeatedly being damaged or killed by winter frosts — then go mainly for reliably tough, hardy plants. Avoid shrubs and perennial plants described as not completely hardy, a little tender, requiring winter protection or a very warm and sheltered site; unless you are prepared to give them special attention and accept possible disappointments.

Where wind exposure is a serious problem, creating shelter should be the long-term aim (*see* 'Hedging and screening', p10). But choosing suitably sturdy and wind-tolerant plants will also help. Avoid tall-growing border plants, which may require time-wasting staking or other support, and shrubs for which catalogues or gardening books recommend a well-sheltered site.

For an exposed coastal garden, plants which are both wind-tolerant and salt-resistant are especially useful — particularly when choosing plants for hedging to take the brunt of the wind and salt spray.

If your garden suffers from the low rainfall levels of the south-east and is also located on a fast-draining dry soil (e.g. sandy or chalky), improving the site and selecting drought-resistant plants and shrubs will help to reduce the labour of summer watering.

Diagram (opposite page): Frost pockets may occur in low-lying valley-bottoms or hollows, and behind barriers which block the flow of cold air down slopes.

1. Camellia japonica variety 'Adolphe Audusson'. In cold northern and inland gardens camellias appreciate as much shelter as possible, to protect their buds and early spring flowers from frost damage.

2. Cistus 'Silver Pink'. The cistus (sun rose) species and varieties are popular but slightly tender shrubs prone to frost damage in severe winters. The colder the garden, the more shelter they need to thrive. A warm site at the base of a sunny wall is ideal.

3. Campanula Poscharskyana: Low-growing rock plants are good for very windy gardens.

2

3

9

Does your garden need hedging or screening for wind

shelter, privacy, or to hide an unattractive view?

All plants appreciate some shelter from the wind, as much as the gardener does. In summer, strong winds dry the soil and speed up water loss from leaves, greatly worsening the effects of prolonged droughts. During severe winter weather, cold easterly winds from the Continent increase frost-damage, freeze-drying resting buds and evergreen leaves by dragging moisture from them while roots are frozen solid in the soil and unable to take up replacement water.

The larger the garden, the taller the sheltering screen needs to be to give good protection throughout its width and length. But a hedge will provide wind shelter up to a distance of 10-20 times its height, so that even a fairly low one will make an appreciable difference in a smaller garden.

Hedge or fence — which to choose?

Solid wooden fences (woven or lapped) are a popular choice for providing instant screening and privacy, but they do have their drawbacks. They are cheaper than walls, but can be more expensive than hedging; they are prone to gale damage in exposed situations; and they are not such efficient wind-breaks as hedges.

Wind which hits a solid fence (or wall) tends to rocket up and over the barrier, causing blustery down-draughts (harmful to plants) immediately on the other side, then whistles across the garden. A hedge, on the other hand, absorbs the wind into its mass of soft foliage, twigs and branches, filtering and slowing the blast. Any gusts of wind which emerge through the other side or over the top are much reduced in force and far less troublesome to garden and gardener alike. Hedges, once established, also provide a more permanent shelter than fences.

I. Cupressocyparis leylandii hedge.

Hedges are therefore far more preferable as wind-breaks in exposed situations, solid fences being better suited to more sheltered sites, or for screening and dividing within larger gardens. The alternative (if you can afford it) is to put up a fence for immediate privacy, and to plant a hedge inside the fence as a longer-term, more attractive and more efficient wind-break replacement.

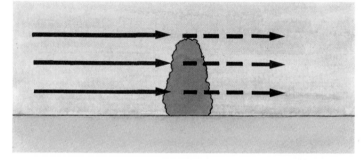

A. Hedges provide excellent wind shelter. They absorb the main force of the wind, filtering it and slowing it down.

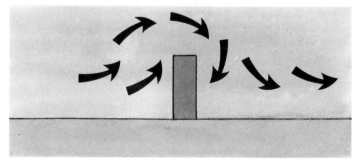

B. Solid walls and fences are less effective as wind-breaks.

Hedges, too, have their drawbacks, the main one being that they need regular clipping once established (but then fences need regular weather-proofing, and eventual replacement) and the fastest-growing hedging plants, which provide the quickest screens, need the most frequent attention.

Once established, hedges also draw large quantities of moisture from the surrounding soil in spring and summer. The most vigorous and thirsty-rooted hedges, such as privet and that immensely popular hedging conifer, *Cupressocyparis leylandii* (the Leyland cypress) can literally suck adjoining borders dry, making it difficult to grow plants close to the base of the hedge. This can be a serious problem if your garden is on the small side and growing space for plants is already scarce; in which case you would be better off planting a less thirsty, slower-growing hedge which will not create problems later on.

If you already have problems with dry soil at the base of a large hedge, where plants struggle to grow, do not despair; there are some drought-resistant plants, shrubs and bulbs which will tolerate such conditions, either in the shade or on the sunny side of a hedge.

2

2. *Armeria maritima (thrift). A tough little plant, ideal for windy gardens.*

3. *Tulipa greigii. Dwarf bulbs are very good.*

To screen off a very obtrusive, unattractive view outside the garden, such as a nearby ugly building, or to provide quick wind-shelter on a very exposed site, a fast-growing hedge will obviously be desirable. But never forget that the most vigorous hedging plants can quickly get out of hand if they are not regularly and correctly cut back. The exceedingly fast-growing Leyland cypress, in particular, will quickly make a very tall hedge, up to 30ft or more in height, if its upward growth is not halted at the required level and kept there by annual trimming. At the same time, the sides will bush out to an amazing degree, gobbling up valuable garden space, if they are not annually trimmed. And once this conifer has formed a fat hedge, reducing its thickness can prove difficult as bare brown patches produced by cutting back the sides are slow to green up again; if cut back really hard, they may never do so.

3

Why are plants alongside hedges, solid fences and walls across a sloping site sometimes more badly damaged by winter frosts than plants elsewhere in the garden?

Walls, hedges and fences normally provide a little shelter from winter cold, especially if they are south-facing. But if you find that the very opposite happens in your garden, the reason may be that cold air is flowing down from higher ground (since cold air is heavier than warm air and will always flow down a slope to lower ground) and that this cold air is collecting in a pool behind the wall, fence or hedge, barring its way across the slope.

Be wary, therefore, of placing a solid barrier all the way across a sloping garden or across its lower boundary, and be particularly wary of creating boxed-in corners at the bottom of a sloping site.

Gaps at each end of a short barrier, for cold air to flow out and away, will help, but for a long screen choose something which won't impede air flow so much — a more open fence made attractive with climbing plants, or a less solid planting of shrubs with gaps to let cold air through. Barriers running up and down the slope are, of course, no problem.

If an existing barrier is causing frost-pocket worries, the only answers are to replace it with a more open screen as above or to create gaps for air-flow. Failing all else, give affected plants and shrubs winter protection.

What are the quickest ways to screen or disguise unattractive features within the garden?

Features which typically benefit from being covered up or otherwise disguised include unsightly walls and outbuildings, obtrusive garages, manhole covers, bare or dilapidated fences, the harsh straight lines of concrete paths and compost heaps.

SHRUBS

Evergreen shrubs are ideal for hiding smaller ugly features like compost heaps and for softening the lines of larger features like outbuildings and garages all the year round. But evergreens (especially the more attractive types) are generally slower-growing than deciduous shrubs and may take some time to make a decent screen.

One solution is to plant fast-growing and bushy deciduous shrubs, such as broom, forsythia, flowering currant, *Lavatera olbia 'Rosea'*, or shrub roses, as close as possible to whatever needs hiding, to provide good summer screening plus some twiggy camouflage in winter and then to plant evergreens in front of them to give year-round cover in the long run. Manhole covers in the garden can be disguised by planting low-growing, spreading evergreen shrubs to trail over them. Ground-hugging spreading conifers are probably the best choice. Heathers, *helianthemums* (rock roses), red-berried *Cotoneaster microphyllus* and the variegated-leaved *Euonymus fortunei* varieties are also good.

The same kinds of low spreading ground-cover plants and shrubs may be used to overlap, disguise and soften the harsh, straight edges of concrete paths, patios, driveways and any other hard-surfaced areas in the garden. But be wary of planting the most wide-spreading types alongside narrow paths, narrow driveways or anywhere else where they may become a nuisance. The most vigorous spreading ground-cover conifers (notably the *Juniperus horizontalis* varieties) and, in particular, the low-growing cotoneaster plants can travel sideways very fast and become a real nuisance. If left to spread far and wide and then cut hard back, they can look very odd and unsightly with their stubby pruned branches.

CLIMBERS AND WALL SHRUBS

Fast-growing climbers and wall shrubs are the answer for hiding and softening unsightly outbuildings, walls and fences. Self-clinging climbers, such as the ivies and Virginia creepers, need no wires or other support once established, as the aerial roots from their stems grip the wall. But they do need some help to get them started. Tying them in to canes or masonry nails, to hold their early growths tight against the wall and prevent their stems from blowing in the wind, makes it easier for them to get an initial grip.

Householders often worry about the damage

1

2

3

4

5

1. Polygonum baldschuanicum (the Russian vine). An extremely fast-growing climber for covering large walls, fences etc. quickly.
2. Rosa filipes 'Kifsgate'. The fastest-growing climbing rose, will rapidly cover the largest of walls; seen here scrambling over a tree stump.
3. Rose 'Nevada'. Vigorous shrub rose useful for fast screening. The large flowers are produced over a long period.
4. Evergreen pyracanthas (the firethorns) provide year-round wall cover, plus bright yellow, orange or red winter berries.
5. Rose 'Zepherine Drouhin'. A vigorous climber which may also be grown as a bush or a/hedge.

that self-clinging climbers may do to their walls. But, provided a wall is in a reasonable condition, with sound brickwork or stonework and mortar, no great harm should be done. It is the dilapidated flaking wall with loose mortar which may be seriously damaged. And you should beware of putting a clinging climber on a rendered wall, where the weight could eventually pull the rendering away.

Be warned, also, that (as with the most vigorous hedging plants) the very fastest-growing climbers, although excellent for rapid screening, can become a nuisance in time. To take a typical example, *Polygonum baldschuanicum* (the Russian vine, or 'mile-a-minute vine') is a popular choice which will quickly smother a small building, wall or fence, growing 6ft or more in a single summer. But it won't necessarily stop when you want it to, as it loves to twine and scramble into nearby shrubs and trees, and needs to be kept constantly in check. Think very carefully before planting this or any other rampant climber in places where growing space is strictly limited. A less strong-growing climber, though it might take a little longer to fill the space, will be less of a worry later.

The most popular and colourful flowering climbers, such as the roses, clematis, and honeysuckles, are non-clinging and must be supported by tying-in to wires, wooden trelliswork or special wall-nails (available from most garden shops). So must the wall-covering shrubs, which are equally useful for disguising ugly features and adding interest to blank walls. But they need less support and attention than the non-clinging climbers, being naturally bushy and more or less self-supporting. These are generally fast-growing evergreen and deciduous shrubs which, if planted in an open border, would make a normal bush. But against a wall or fence, their branches take advantage of the extra support and spread upwards to greater heights. All that is needed in most cases is to tie in some of the main stems when they grow higher and floppier to keep the top of the shrub close to the wall. Regular pruning to remove shoots which are growing outwards away from the wall will encourage plenty of flat, spreading growth sideways and upwards. Most valuable of all are the evergreen wall-covering shrubs, such as the bright winter-berrying *pyracanthas*. These provide solid, year-round cover, and tend to be shrubs which will grow successfully against cold shady walls as well as in sunnier situations.

Do not, however, scorn deciduous climbers and wall shrubs just because they don't retain their leaves all year and therefore seem less desirable for screening purposes. There are few hardy evergreen climbers from which to choose in any case, and a great many of the most attractive climbers and wall-covering shrubs are deciduous. These may lose their leaves in winter, but they give good foliage cover in summer, when the garden is most frequently in use. And even in winter, the mass of branches and twigs offers some softening cover for bare walls and ugly features.

6. Clematis montana rubens. A fast growing climber for quick coverage of walls, fences, outbuildings etc. Spring flowers.
7. Rose 'Zepherine Drouhin'. (close-up). A virtually thornless rose, a good climber with a long flowering season and rich perfume.
8. Clematis 'Nelly Moser'. Free-flowering and popular variety, best in a shady site.

HEDGES

The same argument applies to hedges. For privacy, screening and wind-shelter, an evergreen hedge may seem the obvious choice. But in some situations (e.g. a very small garden or an already shady site) a tall evergreen boundary screen might create a lot of deep and depressing shade in autumn, spring and winter. Deciduous hedges are just as efficient as windbreaks and visual screens as evergreens when you are outside in summer. And in winter, a deciduous hedge (dense and twiggy, thanks to regular trimming) still provides a fair amount of wind-shelter and visual screening even when devoid of leaves; and at the same time it lets sunlight filter through to brighten the garden. Add to that the fact there are some lovely flowering deciduous hedging plants, such as the sweetly perfumed *Rosa rugosa*, for screening plus colourful interest, and you will see that the choice does not have to be evergreens every time for hedges.

1. Berberis stenophylla. Fast growing and will quickly form a handsome evergreen hedge or screen. Flowers in spring.
2. Juniperus communis 'Depressa Aurea'. 3. J. horizontalis. Two fast-spreading prostrate conifers ideal for ground cover.
4. Aubrieta varieties. Good for trailing over retaining walls.

Camellias, rhododendrons and azaleas all prefer some shade from hot summer sunshine, so are perfect choices for gloomy areas of the garden. Remember that all of these need lime-free soil.
5. Camellia williamsii variety 'Donation'. One of the easiest varieties to grow and flower well. Particularly hardy, so a good choice for colder regions.
6. Rhododendron 'Pink Pearl'. An easy and free-flowering hybrid.
7. Rh. 'Elizabeth'. One of the loveliest of the dwarf rhodos.
8. Azalea 'Hinomayo'. Popular dwarf evergreen azalea variety.
9. Azalea Mollis variety. One of the showy deciduous azaleas.

How do you cope with shade problems?

Most plants prefer a sunny site, and many need plenty of sunlight to flower well (and, in the case of most fruits and some vegetables, to crop well). Some plants and shrubs, however, tolerate, or even prefer, semi-shade or light shade — a planting site which is in deep shade (such as that cast by buildings and tall walls) for part of the day or which receives dappled, passing shade from surrounding trees or large shrubs without ever being totally dark and gloomy.

Constant, day-long heavy shade suits only a limited number of plants. Damp shady ground, in which various shade-loving and moisture-loving plants will thrive, is usually a better proposition than ground that is both heavily shaded and very dry, such as the soil underneath the leaf-canopy of large trees or on the shady side of a tall and thirsty-rooted hedge. Yet some plants will survive even there and provide some colour and interest. The answer, as always, is to choose plants to suit the situation.

When making plans, always reserve the sunniest spots for your summer leisure areas (lawn, patio, children's play-area, etc.) and for vegetables and fruits. And never despair of a shady garden. Provided the soil is not too dry, cool shade will allow you to grow to perfection some beautiful shade-loving plants which gardeners in more sun-baked situations would struggle to keep alive.

Grass hates constant shade, and that makes lawns difficult to establish and maintain in good condition in gloomy areas (particularly in the dry shade beneath large trees). In such situations, bald patches and moss tend to be a perpetual irritant. When sowing a new lawn in a shaded or partly shaded spot, therefore, choose one of the shade-tolerant grass-seed mixtures now widely available from garden shops and seed catalogues and prepare the soil especially carefully before sowing. On heavy wet ground (e.g. sticky clay) work into the proposed lawn site plenty of coarse sand (and preferably some peat as well) to lighten the soil and improve drainage. In dry situations, spread peat alone, and work it into the soil to improve its moisture-retention. Rake in a generous dressing of a general fertilizer, such as blood, fish and bone, or a specialized pre-seeding lawn fertilizer, and remember to feed annually to boost growth.

Shady areas of existing lawn which cause worries may be improved in a similar fashion. Over-sow problem areas with a shade-tolerant grass-seed mixture after spiking the turf with a garden fork or specialized lawn spiking tool and raking or brushing into the grass the soil-improving materials already recommended — on heavy soils, lots of coarse sand and some peat, in dry situations, peat alone. And don't forget to feed the lawn.

Do you have a problem soil — and how would you recognize it?

The three major soil types which cause problems are heavy clays, sandy soils and shallow, chalky soils, as you will very soon realize if you try to garden on one of them.

Clays are heavy to dig, very sticky when wet (clods cling annoyingly to boots and tools) and rock-hard when dried-out in summer. They are difficult to break down from large, solid clods into a fine, crumbly soil desirable for planting and sowing. And they are very slow-draining, remaining water-logged (often with puddles lying on the surface) for long periods after heavy rain.

Sandy soils are virtually the opposite: fine-textured, very free-draining and easily worked, even after heavy rain. But they are exceptionally quick to dry out in spring and summer, making drought a constant worry. Such soils also tend to be acid, and they are usually short of essential plant foods, resulting in generally slow plant growth.

Shallow, chalky soils are unmistakable: a thin layer of fast-draining top-soil, containing white chalk lumps, overlying virtually solid chalk. As with sandy soils, the major worry is drought, since the thin top-soil quickly becomes parched during dry spells. The other important point is that, being lime-rich, chalk soils are not suitable for lime-hating plants, such as rhododendrons, azaleas and camellias.

These difficult soils may all be improved to make them less troublesome, and for vegetable growing some soil-improvement is generally essential if you are to get good crops. However, soil-improvement on a wide scale throughout the whole of the ornamental garden can be very time-consuming and expensive, especially where large areas are involved. It should always be coupled with sensible selection of plants to suit the soil-type, going along with the prevailing conditions rather than constantly struggling against them.

1, 2 and *3. Azaleas produce a brilliantly colourful spring display rivalled only for sheer flower power by the most exotic of the rhododendron hybrids. The dwarf evergreen azaleas also make excellent plants for growing in tubs to add colour to shady corners of the garden. Be sure to use a lime-free 'ericaceous' potting compost when planting these and other lime-hating shrubs (such as the rhododendrons and camellias) in pots and tubs. In the garden they must have lime-free soil.*

3

4

5

4. Primula japonica. *5.* Primula florindae. *The border primulas are useful plants for colour in late spring and early summer. All prefer shady situations. Others to look out for include the popular P. denticulata (drumstick primula), P. beesiana (purple flowers), P. belleyana (orange) and P. sikkimensis (the giant Himalayan cowslip).*

17

What can be done to make steeply sloping gardens

more manageable and attractive?

Unfortunately there is little that can be done to reduce the wear on the poor gardener's legs in a very steep garden! Except, if space allows, to plan your paths so that they wind their way up the slope from side to side, at a gentle gradient, rather than lay them straight up the slope. Winding paths also make for more interesting garden walks.

TERRACES

From the visual point of view, steep gardens can look quite spectacular and are somewhat easier to make interesting (with terraces, retaining walls, sloping rock gardens, ponds and cascading waterfalls, etc.) than many a flatter garden site. Apart from adding variety to the garden layout, terracing with retaining walls to provide at least some flat areas will make gardening operations easier. And it will allow you to establish a lawn on a level (or, at least, a more level) site or to lay a patio for sitting-out. It is particularly useful to have a level, terraced area for vegetable-growing in a sloping garden. This makes regular cultivation of the soil easier and prevents the soil from being washed down the plot by heavy rains, so that over the years you do not find the solid depth at the top end gradually decreasing.

When building retaining walls, leave planting holes for trailing plants to add interest and colour to the face of the wall.

The soil on steep, south-facing slopes tends to dry out fast in spring and summer, due to the sunny aspect and the rapid drainage of rainwater down a sloping site. Drought problems are particularly serious on a vegetable or fruit plot, especially if the soil is sandy or chalky. In such circumstances, terracing to create level areas will reduce the surface run-off of rainwater and stop soil-drying sunlight from hitting the ground head-on, making for moister summer soil conditions and reducing the need for watering. This will benefit ornamental plants and, more important, will make a great difference to vegetable crops.

1. Thuja occidentalis variety 'Rheingold'. One of the very best golden-foliage dwarf conifer varieties.
2. Arabis albida. A popular rock plant for growing in walls.
3. Chamaecyparis pisifera variety 'Boulevard'. Superb blue conifer.
4. Lavatera olbia 'Rosea'. A very fast growing shrub which flowers all summer long.
5. Oenothera missouriensis. Lovely trailing rock plant which flowers non-stop throughout summer.
6. Dianthus 'Mrs Sinkins'. 7. D. 'Doris'. Two popular garden 'pinks' which need well-drained soil and are often planted on rock gardens.

Shady, north-facing slopes, on the other hand, suffer from a shortage of sunlight, notably in autumn, winter and spring. Here, terracing will level the ground out so that sunshine hits the soil at less of a shallow angle, increasing its warming effect on the ground. This is particularly important for vegetable plots, where faster soil-warming in spring makes earlier sowings possible and more sun in late summer and early autumn extends cropping. An additional benefit of terracing is that dry-built retaining walls, with soil packed into the larger gaps and cracks for plants, or mortared walls with holes left specially for plants, will allow you to create handsome wall-gardens full of colour and interest. Trailing rock plants are especially suited to such situations. Existing retaining walls devoid of planting holes may be softened and disguised with spreading plants and shrubs, sited in the soil behind, to spill over the top and tumble downwards.

ROCK GARDENS

Rock gardens always look particularly 'right' on a steep slope, exactly the situation where natural rock-outcrops (which rock gardeners seek to imitate) would normally occur. They are also just the kind of site where alpine plants would grow in their native mountains. Rock plants require well-drained soil which doesn't become too wet in winter, so that steep sites suit them perfectly. Heathers and slow-growing or dwarf conifers also look good on slopes, whether as part of a rock garden or in a heather and conifer scheme of their own (dwarf conifers appreciate well-drained soil as much as the rock plants with which they combine so well).

SHELTER

Bear in mind that gardens on slopes are more exposed to wind than those on flatter ground. Providing good wind-shelter is usually a major priority, but it is sometimes difficult to achieve on a very steep slope. The natural instinct is to plant very fast-growing hedges (such as the *leylandii* conifer) for a tall screen, or to put up fences for immediate protection. But remember that solid wooden fences are less efficient as wind-breaks than hedges and that very tall, strong-growing hedges may create too much shade in small gardens on north-facing slopes as well as make the soil in adjoining borders too dry. Aim to achieve a balanced compromise — hedges for wind-shelter, but not too strong-growing and tall, and a selection of suitable wind-tolerant plants for the garden.

2

3

4

5

6

7

19

How can you add interest to a flat garden site?

This is really a question of general layout and style (*see* section on style, p.28), but it is worthwhile mentioning the various ways in which you can add interest to a level site through variations in height and scale.

Most obviously, you can landscape the site, excavating to create shady dells and sunken gardens for ponds and moisture-loving plants, while building up the level in other areas for shrub-planted banks and rock gardens. Major landscaping is, however, mainly a recipe for large areas and has its limitations in smaller gardens. Where space is limited, you can still introduce some variations in soil level into a flat site, but resist the temptation to try anything too ambitious, which may look ridiculous in a small area.

Rock gardens have long been a popular choice as raised features to break up a very flat site. Just as good, and increasingly popular these days, are

Left and above: Rock gardens and raised beds are ideal features for adding interest to a flat garden site, introducing variety of ground level. They need not be raised up very high to look good and be ideal homes for alpines, dwarf bulbs and dwarf conifers.

Below: Thuja orientalis 'Aurea Nana' is one of the best dwarf golden-foliage dwarf conifers. Right: Juniperus virginiana 'Skyrocket'. A handsome conifer which grows into a very narrow column shape, making it a good choice for small gardens.

What special problems does a small garden pose?

The most obvious difficulty with a small garden is the limited growing space. Resist the temptation to plant too many of the fastest-growing and space-hungry plants and shrubs in an attempt to fill the garden quickly. Go mainly for neater-growing things, so that you can squeeze plenty of variety and interest into what space you have. Do not let this become an obsession, however, as a few larger shrubs and plants are essential for variety of height and scale. A garden full of miniatures and dwarfs will be flat and boring.

low-walled raised beds, which are suitable for growing rock plants (thanks to the increased drainage in a raised bed), as well as a wide range of other plants and shrubs.

These features may be built up with soil removed from the intended sites of ponds, patios, paths, sheds, etc. (It is generally necessary to excavate some depth of soil before laying hardcore or sand foundations for garden buildings and flagged or concreted areas). If necessary, the volume may be increased by the addition of peat (which will improve the soil at the same time). Take care, when excavating soil to make raised beds and rock gardens, that you do not dig so deep as to mix poor-quality sub-soil (e.g. stony rubbish or heavy clay) with the good top-soil. Top-soil used in creating such raised features should be carefully sieved to remove all weed roots. Alternatively, raised beds may be filled with bags of peat-based or soil-based potting compost.

Another way to disguise the sheer flatness of a level site is the careful planning of planting schemes, grouping plants of different sizes in such a way that they produce gradual variations and contrasts of height and scale. Build up from low plants at the front and sides of a border to taller plants at the back and in the middle. And place tall plants amongst the smaller ones for contrast.

TREES

In particular, choose trees for small gardens very carefully indeed, checking up on eventual height and spread to make sure that they will not out-grow the garden and create problems of shade and dry soil. Beware most of all the very large forest trees such as horse chestnut, beech, and the larger conifers; and avoid thirsty-rooted trees like willows, birches, and poplars, which can suck the garden dry with their far-reaching surface roots.

There are plenty of small trees suitable for restricted spaces, but even among these, the smaller the garden, the more carefully you should choose. Flowering cherries, for example, are widely recommended for small gardens, but only the neatest types suit a really small plot. Be especially wary of the very popular and widely-planted dark-pink, double-flowered variety, *Kanzan*, a strong-growing tree which can reach a considerable size in time.

FRUIT AND VEGETABLES

Squeezing fruit and vegetables into a tiny garden alongside ornamental plants and shrubs can sometimes pose a problem. It may be better to apply for a local authority allotment. Following a recent wave of popularity, when they were often difficult to obtain, more and more allotments are now reportedly falling vacant in many parts of the country, and you may be lucky enough to get one.

Growing the more attractive fruits and vegetables in borders among the flowering plants and shrubs, in the old cottage-garden style, is also becoming increasingly popular. Suitable, handsome-looking subjects include dwarf bush apples, strawberries (an excellent border edging), rhubarb, dwarf bush tomatoes, scarlet-flowered runner beans (grown on 'wigwams' of garden canes), sweet corn (like a handsome ornamental grass), courgettes and outdoor bush cucumbers (pretty yellow flowers and attractive leaves), carrots (frilly foliage for a border edging) and, of course, useful and attractive herbs of all kinds (thyme, parsley, rosemary, chives etc.) Dwarf bush apples are especially suited to small gardens, and are becoming increasingly popular. For the neatest bushes, choose apple varieties grafted on to the dwarfing rootstock M27. This produces tidy bushes just 4-5ft high, which need little pruning and yield large fruits soon after planting. Some crops may also be grown on walls or fences, providing a feature as attractive as an

1

2

3

5

6

4

1. Acer griseum *(the paperbark maple). A slow growing small tree ideal for restricted spaces. Beautiful peeling red-brown bark and brilliant autumn colour.*

2. A. palmatum *'Dissectum' (cut-leaved Japanese maple). One of the best small shrubs for bright autumn leaf colour. The feathery foliage looks good all the year round.*

3. A. palmatum *'Dissectum Atropurpureum'. Same as above, but with purple foliage, turning a brighter purple-red in autumn.*

4. Prunus *'Amanogawa' (flowering cherry). A narrowly upright growing cherry variety popular with owners of small gardens.*

5. P. 'Tai Haku' *(flowering cherry). The largest-flowered of all the ornamental cherries.*

6. Juniperus squamata *'Blue Star'. A superb dwarf conifer.*

ornamental climber, with the bonus of vitamin-rich food fresh from the garden. Consider scarlet runner beans, blackberries (preferably a thornless variety), fan-trained pears, plums and cherries; even peaches, apricots or an outdoor grape variety can flourish on a sunny wall in a sheltered garden.

SCREENING AND SHADE

Some general garden problems are often much more troublesome in small gardens. Ugly features within the garden are always obvious and demand early screening, and shade may be particularly difficult to escape. Do think carefully before using vigorous growing shrubs and climbers for screening in a restricted area, as they can quickly get out of hand. And overgrown hedges, casting too much shade and sucking borders dry with their roots, are a common trouble. Be wary of planting large trees and too many large shrubs and consider your choice of hedging material very carefully. Try to resist being tempted by the most vigorous hedging plants (such as the *leylandii* conifer and privet). Choose something less overpowering and difficult to contain.
Make full use of walls and fences to support climbing plants for added colour and interest in a small area. And bear in mind that climbers may also be trained up into trees and large shrubs for a double display in the same growing space; the best choices for this purpose are the large-flowered clematis hybrids and the honeysuckles. Beware of planting vigorous climbers to grow into small trees, and always give the tree or large shrub a couple of years to become established before training any climber up into its branches.

CONTAINERS AND RAISED BEDS

Containers can be of immense value in small gardens, especially paved courtyards. Consider all the different possibilities: hanging baskets for summer colour; window boxes for seasonal displays in spring and summer; and tubs or troughs for seasonal colour or permanent displays on patios and other hard areas.
A rock garden, or a raised bed planted with rock plants, is an excellent feature for a small garden. Tidy-growing alpine plants allow you to squeeze a great variety of colour and interest into even the tiniest of planting areas. They also look good with the dwarf conifers and dwarf bulbs that are equally good choices for restricted spaces. Raised beds (whether planted with alpines or other plants and shrubs) and

rock gardens are perfect features for creating variety of height in a small level garden, helping to break up the flatness of the site. And the low walls of raised beds make handy seats if space for garden furniture is limited.

GAPS AND CRACKS

Look for the less obvious planting spaces in a small garden. Plants in gaps between paving slabs, in gaps in dry retaining walls or in planting holes built into mortared retaining walls, will help you to squeeze in extra colour and interest. When laying paving or building retaining walls, remember to deliberately leave

planting gaps if you want to make use of this extra growing space. Better still, put in plants as you lay the slabs or build the wall, so that you can prepare the soil and plant more carefully and easily than you could once the paving or wall is finished. With close-fitting paving, create planting gaps by knocking a corner off a slab here and there as you lay them. Alternatively, seeds of suitable spreading plants may be sown into cracks. Remember that plants in paving must be low-growing spreaders which will not be a nuisance to step over; and they should be tough plants which will not mind the occasional trampling.

1

2

1. Narcissus 'Tete-a-Tete'. All the dwarf daffodil varieties are excellent choices for small gardens, their neater foliage taking up less space after flowering than the large leaves of the tall trumpet types. This is a charming variety, bearing two flowers to a stem. Others to look out for include 'February Gold', 'Peeping Tom', 'Jack Snipe' and 'Dove Wings'.
2. Magnolia stellata. A superb slow growing shrub for small gardens. Stunning in March–April when the fragrant starry flowers smother the bare branches. It flowers freely even as a young specimen such as this one.

3. Rhododendron 'Elizabeth'. One of the lovliest of the dwarf rhododendrons, all of which are good choices for small gardens. But remember that they need lime-free soil.

4. R. 'Cilpinense'. Another popular dwarf rhodo, noted for its early flowers (March) and neat bushy habit. Best in a well-sheltered spot to protect the blooms from weather damage.

5. Magnolia stellata. The free flowering habit of this beautiful shrub when young is demonstrated on the opposite page. Here is the magnificient display you can expect from a mature specimen.

6. Potentilla fruticosa 'Red Ace'. Potentillas are good shrubs for small gardens, neat growing and flowering non-stop throughout summer.

7. Fuchsia 'Mrs Popple'. The same applies to the hardy fuchsias.

3

6

4

7

What is the best way to tackle a neglected and

overgrown garden?

Should you find yourself taking charge of a neglected garden, full of weeds and overgrown trees, shrubs and hedges, do not be in too much of a hurry to rip out, dig up and hack down everything in sight. Who knows what beautiful plants and shrubs may be hiding in that tangle of weeds and branches — or under the ground. Get on with urgent tasks like weeding and grass-mowing as quickly as possible. But the longer you delay starting any major clearance or replanting plans, the more chance you give the garden to reveal hidden secrets and surprises.

You might discover bulbs and herbaceous plants which were resting below ground when you first arrived, and which could have been damaged in the rush to dig and replant, or unrecognized shrubs and climbers which turn out to be stunning beauties when flowering time comes round (at which time it should prove easier to identify them and check on the best way to prune and care for them).

Time spent in getting to know a new garden before rushing into action is never time wasted. It gives you a chance not only to investigate the existing plants, but to note over the months (and the seasons) what the soil is like, how the weather affects the garden, and any other possible problems; all useful experience which may well affect your plans and which will help you to avoid mistakes.

1

1. Buddleia davidii (butterfly bush). A popular fast growing shrub which can quickly become overgrown if not regularly pruned. Always check the exact pruning requirements of overgrown shrubs before cutting them back. As a general rule, those shrubs which flower in winter and spring, on the previous year's growth, are best pruned as soon as possible after flowering. Those which bloom in summer and autumn, on young shoots, are best cut back in early spring.
2. Lilium regale (regal lily).
3. Crocus chrysanthus 'E.P. Bowles'. If you're renovating an overgrown garden, remember that, depending on the time of the year, there may be bulbs and herbaceous plants resting below ground. Take care with the spade.
4. Phlox drummondii (annual phlox). Annuals will provide instant colour in a newly-cleared garden while you establish more permanent/plants.

2

PRUNING

Always check the pruning requirements of overgrown shrubs and climbers before chopping them back or giving them an all-over trim. It is so easy to spoil a lovely shrub, destroying its natural shape or the following season's flower display, by pruning in the wrong way or at the wrong time of year. Some shrubs may be rejuvenated by cutting all growths back hard, but a great many others demand more gentle treatment, thinning out the oldest and longest branches to reduce their size and make room for younger and shorter flowering shoots. It also pays to check how and when to cut back and trim overgrown hedges, because they, too, vary in their requirements.

REMOVING TREES AND SHRUBS

When the complete removal of shrubs or trees is essential, it is best to remove as much of the root system as possible, in addition to the top growth. Leaving stumps with rotting roots in the soil may provide the perfect home for some very common and troublesome root-killing fungi (such as honey-fungus), which can then spread to other shrubs, trees and hedges in the garden with disastrous results.

Do not cut trees and shrubs down to a very short stump before trying to rip out the roots. Leave a taller stump, so that when you attack the roots with spade and axe, hauling on the tall stump will help to lever the roots out of the ground with more ease.

Bear in mind that felling is not always the answer. If a tree or large shrub is causing trouble (such as creating excessive shade, blocking an attractive view, or taking up too much space with low-sweeping branches), removing lower branches to produce a clean trunk, or thinning the branches to produce a more open effect, may solve the problem. Felling or lopping small ornamental trees and fruit trees may be within the abilities of the gardener, but large trees should always be tackled by experts. Even individual branches can be deceptively heavy and dangerously unpredictable. Tree surgeons are also the best people to deal with large and stubborn tree stumps. They have noisy, but effective, machines which will literally chew up stumps into chips and sawdust. If you must deal with a large stump yourself, try burning it away by repeatedly building bonfires over it.

If you decide to leave tree stumps to rot in the ground, fat ugly stumps may be camouflaged with evergreen ground-cover plants such as ivies and spreading conifers. Alternatively, leave a taller stump, and you will have a support for climbing plants such as roses and clematis to ramble over.

WEEDS

Weed control should always be one of the first priorities in neglected gardens. After a short period of neglect, you may have chiefly annual weeds to cope with; following prolonged neglect, there may be a mass of deep-rooted perennial weeds, such as dandelions, docks, bindweed, nettles and perhaps even tree saplings and brambles.

Annual weeds may be simply chopped off with a hoe, but it is vitally important to remove or kill the roots of perennial weeds, which will become an endless worry if ignored or hoed-off at ground level before you start planting. Digging and removing deep perennial weed roots by hand is the traditional method, but for large weedy areas you may prefer to choose chemical control.

Deep-rooted bindweed (left) and invasive creeping couch grass (right) are typical examples of troublesome perennial weeds

Make sure that you also remove or kill the roots of any tree seedlings and, most particularly, the roots of any brambles, which may quickly sprout new growth if left in the ground. Persistent regrowth from brambles, tree roots and stumps may also be chemically controlled, but, wherever possible, manual root removal is the quickest and best solution.

LAWNS

Overgrown and neglected lawns should be carefully mown to start with. Set the mower blades high for the first few cuts, to avoid shaving the long grass to its roots and killing it in patches. Allow the turf time to recover between the initial cuts, and gradually lower the blades to cut the grass finer and finer. This will discourage any coarse-growing grasses which have seeded into the lawn, while encouraging the finer lawn grass to re-establish itself. Feeding with specialized lawn fertilizers will also help to rejuvenate neglected areas.

whose roots should always be killed off or dug out before you plant.

4

3

What special problems should you look out for in a new and empty garden?

Many of the general questions raised throughout this chapter may apply to a brand new, unplanted garden and should be carefully considered and taken into account before you rush into buying or planting. Some may be particularly relevant, such as a total lack of wind shelter, numerous soil problems or weeds.

After clearing any builder's rubble and debris from the surface of the site, the soil should always be your first consideration. Is it one of the problem soils discussed in this chapter? If so, how can it be improved, and what plants will best suit it?

Is there any buried builder's rubble which needs to be removed before planting? Check most carefully close to the house, where all kinds of rubbish may have been trampled into the ground.

Has the soil been badly compacted by heavy machinery and builders' boots? Soil that has been trampled down hard or squashed into ruts by tyres should be deeply dug, forked, or Rotavated to return it to a crumblier and better-drained state. Compacted soil is very slow to drain and therefore susceptible to water-logging and surface puddles; plants hate it. Look out for areas where poor sub-soil (e.g. lumps of stony or sticky clay rubbish) has been mixed up with the good top-soil by the builder's digging and bulldozing operations. If you find that this has happened, try to remove as many as possible of the poor-quality sub-soil clods as you dig and plant. If the problem is severe, improve the soil as you plant with peat and other soil-enriching materials.

Watch out also for areas with only a very thin layer of top-soil overlaying poor sub-soil; the builders may well have bulldozed the soil to one side at some point and not re-spread it evenly (or perhaps not even put all of it back). Patches of thin soil may be improved with soil skimmed from deeper areas in the garden. In severe cases you may have to buy extra top-soil or treat what you have with peat and similar materials as you plant.

Weed-clearing should be your next priority. Be sure to remove or kill the roots of perennial weeds, especially such deep-rooted monsters as bindweed, dock and dandelion. Even tiny scraps of root left in the soil may eventually resprout and cause endless trouble in your planted borders. Take special care with sites intended for rock gardens, as deep-rooted weeds are a particular menace among tiny rock plants.

Resist the desire to plant hedges or put up fencing immediately, no matter how windy or short on privacy the garden may be. Consider the pros and cons of hedging and fencing raised above, and think carefully about the choice of hedging material to suit the size of the garden, the soil and the situation. Bear in mind the problems that very fast-growing tall hedges may cause in a small garden: extra work keeping them within bounds, excessive shade, and borders made too dry by vigorous hedge roots.

The state of the soil may also need investigating and improving before any hedging plants are put in. Hedges are important, and if you want a healthy and fast-growing one, you need to be sure that the soil conditions are right. Plant a hedge into poor, unimproved soil, and you will be in for years of frustration — slow, sickly growth and patchy screening due to plant losses. Do the job properly. Dig a trench and break up the sub-soil in the base to ensure good drainage. Then fill in with soil enriched with peat or compost and compound fertiliser.

How should you go about planning or improving the garden layout?

The first step in garden design (whether you are planning a new garden or altering an established one) should always be to get your plans down on paper — no matter how simple you may think your basic scheme is. Measure out the garden as accurately as possible, preferably with a tape measure or, failing that, in shoe-lengths or strides. Then draw up a map with everything to scale (square-ruled graph paper will come in handy). Mark all existing features, including the good and bad points: sunny areas and shady areas; ugly features and views in need of screening and attractive views that you do not want to block with tall-growing shrubs or trees; boundaries which need screening for wind shelter and privacy; south and west boundaries where you should not block out too much sunshine. Now you can start devising your layout and planting schemes. As you formulate your plans, keep returning outdoors, strolling around and trying to imagine how things will look after a few years of growth. In particular, try to imagine how large shrubs and trees will be after ten years or more, and whether they might cause future problems (such as shading a sunny lawn or patio or blocking a nice outlook).

View the garden at various times of day, and on different days, to note how shade moves around and affects all parts of the garden and how differing wind-directions affect the garden. Bear in mind that in Great Britain the prevailing strong winds during the summer are mainly from the south-west, and that in winter it is the biting north-easterlies which cause most damage to plants. Boundaries facing in these directions will probably be the most urgently in need of screening.

Your first priority should be to choose sites for lawns, patios and other leisure areas; and also for the vegetable and fruit plot and the greenhouse, if you plan to have these. All of them should be in the sunniest situations possible. Take care not to place trees or large shrubs where they may eventually cast excessive shade over these sunny areas. Bear in mind, also, the effect that tall hedging may have on these vital spaces and choose your hedging plants, and plan maximum hedge-heights, accordingly. Beds and borders should then be planned around these basic features, noting any shady areas, such as borders and walls which will require special plant selections.

Should you choose a particular garden style?

Before starting, you ought to have at least a basic idea of what kind of garden style you are aiming for: formal, informal, cottage-garden or 'wild' garden.

Once you have decided upon the style, design and layout of your new or revised garden the first and most important step is to get your plans down on paper. Measure out the garden as accurately as possible and then draught-up a simple map (opposite), preferably on graph paper, with everything drawn to scale. This will enable you to plan your garden more efficiently and help you to visualize more clearly what it will eventually look like. Choose sites for dominant garden features first, such as lawns, patios, ponds, greenhouses, vegetable and fruit plots, plan flower beds, borders, hedges or bushes around them. Take care also to situate these features in the most advantageous positions.

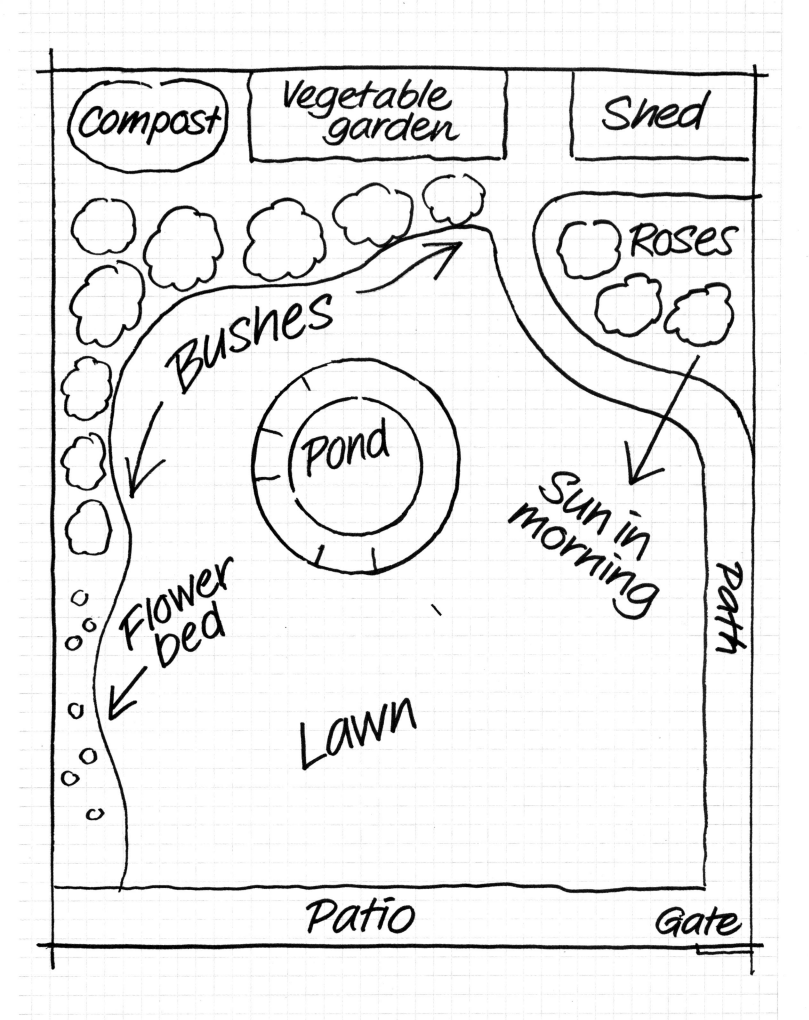

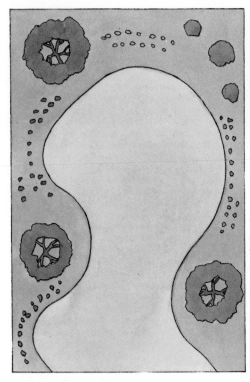

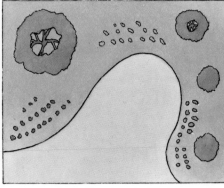

FORMAL GARDENS

Formal gardens are laid out in more or less geometric shapes, with designs incorporating a pattern of circular, square, oblong or triangular beds and borders. This style is often chosen when intricate bedding schemes are planned for spring and summer colour, the gardener creating different effects each year with temporary plants such as annuals, tender perennials, bulbs and hardy bedding plants. It is a style suited to herb gardens and formal plantings of hybrid tea and floribunda roses. Enclosed courtyards and small gardens around modern houses are also frequently designed in an up-to-date formal fashion: geometric designs of paving or gravel, broken up and given added interest and variety with formally-shaped raised beds, geometric pools and container-grown plants and shrubs.

INFORMAL GARDENS

An informal garden style is the most popular choice, particularly for the average-size suburban garden. Its popularity is due to its adaptability to virtually all situations, sizes and shapes of garden. It also helps to disguise the hemmed-in squareness and straight boundaries of the average garden.

The basic style has a more-or-less central lawn, surrounded by gently curving borders planted with a mixture of evergreen and deciduous shrubs, hardy perennial plants and bulbs and, usually, some temporary bedding plants for extra colour in summer.

Too many straight lines are avoided and paths wind and curve in sympathy with the borders. Curving borders and paths distract your eye from the straight lines and square shape of the garden boundary, while informal shrub groupings (with climbers behind, on walls or fences) help further to break up the rectangular monotony of the garden perimeter. Mixed border plantings, including a good sprinkling of evergreens, intermingling with plants and shrubs for different seasons, ensure colour and interest throughout the year, without too many bare winter patches.

COTTAGE-GARDENS

Cottage-style gardening is an increasingly fashionable idea, thanks to its romantic links with the past. In practice, this style is not much different from the informal garden style; it is simply less planned and more informal giving it a seemingly haphazard appearance.

Lawns generally play a less central and important role, and they may be missing altogether, replaced by extra-wide borders or beds, through which run paths straight or winding, wide or narrow. The beds are packed tight with a mixture of all kinds of plants: shrubs, evergreen and deciduous, climbers, bush roses, hardy perennial plants, bulbs, temporary bedding plants, and kitchen herbs — all happily allowed to grow into and through one another, with the minimum of trimming and cutting back, to form a solid mass of colour and foliage.

In a true cottage-garden, some of the more attractive vegetables and fruits may be planted among the flowers: scarlet runner beans on cane 'wigwams', standard-stemmed fruit trees, border edgings of strawberries or curly-leaved parsley, rhubarb patches, courgettes, cucumbers, dwarf bush tomatoes, and so on.

Emphasis is usually on the more traditional, 'old-fashioned' cottage-garden plants, such as roses, honeysuckle, lavender, lupins, Michaelmas daisies, Madonna lilies, crown imperials, pinks and carnations, primroses, pansies and violas, snap-dragons, Sweet William and wallflowers — plus any other shrubs, plants or bulbs which you think will look right. You do not have to be a purist, insisting on only the most 'old-fashioned' plants. Do, however, take care with conifers (especially the dwarf types) most of which can look rather 'modern' for the cottage-garden style (with the notable exception of the handsome yews).

WILD GARDENS

Wild gardening is not to everyone's taste. But more and more of today's gardeners are setting aside at least a corner of their plot as a small, wild 'nature reserve' — a corner less tidily maintained and free from chemical sprays — to provide a natural habitat for garden wildlife. In a large garden, this may be the answer to the problem of what to do with neglected overgrown areas, steep banks and similar worrying sites.

Wild flowers are sown or planted, and grass left uncut, until late summer to allow them to seed. Self-sown 'weeds' which benefit butterflies (e.g. nettles) and other harmless insects, or which are attractive in flower, are less ruthlessly uprooted than in a normal garden. Thickets of evergreen and deciduous shrubs provide roosts and nesting sites for birds, plus winter food, if they are of the berry-producing sorts.

It need not be purely a matter of environment-conscious wildlife preservation – important as that is, with the countryside disappearing at the present rate and wildlife endangered by crop-spraying and the destruction of natural hedgerow habitats. There is a great deal of more selfish pleasure to be had from a corner filled with beautiful wild flowers, which attracts birds, butterflies and other fascinating creatures into your garden.

Many seed catalogues and garden shops now offer extensive ranges of wildflower seeds, and sometimes growing plants as well. Choose carefully to suit the site (shady or sunny, dry or moist) and, for the best results, prepare the soil as you would for garden plants before sowing wildflower seeds. In a large wild garden you may, of course, also introduce some suitably natural-looking garden plants for extra colour and interest.

In a large garden, it may well be possible to incorporate a number of styles, planning separate and distinct areas in different ways according to which styles you feel would best suit the several parts of the garden — perhaps a more formal arrangement of paving and geometric beds close to the house, leading to more distant informal lawns and borders, and finally to a wild or semi-wild area. In a very small garden, however, it is better to stick more or less to one basic style throughout. Otherwise, the garden can begin to look very 'bitty' and cluttered.

Opposite page: Curving borders help to disguise the boxed-in square look of the average garden. Take care to keep the layout bold and simple. Too many kinks and curves in border edges will only create a fussy look.

1. Geranium sanguineum (bloody cranesbill). Hardy perennials like these are indispensable in any garden scheme, to provide permanent interest year after year. Along with shrubs, they are the 'backbone' of the modern garden. 2. Berberis darwinii, a handsome small evergreen shrub. 3. Dwarf Rhododendron variety 'Blue Tit'. 4. Magnolia stellata in a woodland garden setting.

What are the basics of good garden design?

It is most important, especially in a small garden, to avoid a cluttered and fussy design which tries to cram too many little beds and special features into a limited space. A bolder and simpler layout, with cleaner lines, will look better: fewer, but larger, beds or borders and just one or two stunning special features (such as a pond or rock garden).

Try to create a variety of ground-levels, especially on a very flat site. Slopes may be enhanced by terracing with retaining walls; and level gardens by introducing raised beds and rock gardens into the overall scheme. Aim also for contrasts of height and scale in your planting schemes. Avoid grouping together plants which are all very similar in height — a sure recipe for a flat and boring view.

Remember that informal, curving borders (and winding paths) are the best recipe for disguising the straight boundaries and the hemmed-in squareness of the average garden. Curving borders may enhance oddly-shaped gardens, their undulations helping to disguise sharp, angular corners. Do not, however, be tempted to make the edges of informal borders too full of little kinks and bends; the end result will be over-fussy (and make mowing difficult where the borders edge on to a lawn). Go for bold, sweeping curves, especially in a small garden, where space for intricate patterns is strictly limited.

Bear in mind that well-planned, mixed borders (with shrubs, perennial plants, bulbs and bedding plants all intermingled) can provide year-round colour and interest. More selective beds and borders devoted to single-season displays (such as seasonal beddings; formal rose-bush plantings and purely herbaceous borders) can be bare and uninteresting in winter. Seek to achieve a good balance of deciduous shrubs and herbaceous plants for their flowers, and for their changing appearance throughout the seasons (including autumn leaf-tints), plus evergreens for year-round foliage. And do not forget to select plants for colour and interest in all seasons of the year, not just for spring and summer; include at least a few that flower in autumn and winter as well.

What basic mistakes should you avoid?

Always choose your plants according to the situation — shady or sunny, dry or moist, exposed or sheltered, limy soil or non-limy soil. Check individual plant requirements in catalogues and gardening reference books to make sure that you are not putting them in the wrong places. Take care to give trees, shrubs and plants enough room to grow. Check on

4

5

Line drawing (opposite page):
Aim for a wide variety of
plant heights, shapes and
foliage textures in your plantings.
1. Mahonia aquifolium
2. Anemone japonica
3. Phlox subulata
4. Viburnum tinus 'Eve Price'
5. Narcissus 'February Gold'
6. Philadelphus 'Belle Etoile'

6

their ultimate sizes and recommended planting distances; and remember that their spread is at least as important as their height.

Be sure to site sitting-out areas and lawns, vegetable plots and greenhouses in the sunniest possible situations, and make sure that your shrubs and trees will not eventually cause excessive shade in these areas. Try not to cut out too much general sunlight with trees, large shrubs and tall hedges on boundaries facing south and west. Shade cast in the morning from east boundaries is never much of a problem, and your garden will benefit from all the shelter you can give it from freezing easterly winds in winter. However, take care as you do not want to lose your afternoon sun — or your evening sun, when sitting out late in summer can be such a pleasure.

Avoid blocking attractive views with trees, shrubs or hedges which will eventually grow too tall. A garden boundary with a nice view, but which needs wind-shelter, might be better planted with a carefully planned selection of shrubs of varying heights, rather than with a solid hedge, thus providing some tall-growing wind protection, while preserving views through the gaps.

Beware of placing large trees too close to the house. Their roots may damage the foundations and their branches may cut out light from windows. Similarly, avoid planting trees and very large shrubs too close to drains, sewers and water mains, which strong roots may crack and penetrate. The chances of tree root-damage depends greatly on the type of soil. On clay soils, prone to rapid shrinkage and cracking in dry spells, tree roots close to a wall will increase the soil-drying and soil-shrinking effect, making subsidence more likely. On lighter, non-clay soils, tree roots near buildings should be somewhat less of a worry. To be on the safe side, plant trees at a distance from the house equal to their ultimate height, especially on clay soils. Trees with very far-reaching, thirsty roots, such as poplars and large weeping willows, should be kept as far away as possible from house walls and underground pipes — and should be banned entirely from small gardens.

Shrubs and climbers close to walls (or against walls) should not normally be a cause for worry, as they generally have far smaller and less penetrating root systems than trees. The same goes for slow-growing conifers, which never reach a great height and may be considered as shrubs. On a heavy clay soil, however, it might be advisable to avoid placing very large and vigorous shrubs up against house walls (especially if the house has a history of subsidence).

Do not be hasty to remove an existing large tree which you feel may be too close to the house. It may not be posing any real threat to your property. And the disturbance and effect on the soil of its removal (especially on a clay soil) may in itself cause damage to the house wall — not to mention the possibility of a serious accident if a large tree is tackled by someone without professional experience. Call in a tree surgeon for expert advice and, if necessary, to do the job.

You should not, in any case, fell a mature tree without very good cause. Is it really as much of a problem as you think? And will it leave a glaring gap in the garden, so that you will miss it the moment it is gone? Where excessive shade or a blocked view are the worries, perhaps some lopping and thinning of the branches may help. Once again, seek expert advice before making your decision.

Most important of all, avoid the very basic mistake of rushing too quickly into any major garden planting or replanting schemes. First try to envisage exactly what your planned garden will look like when mature. This will help you to spot potential mistakes.

33

THE SOIL

What are the ideal soil conditions for gardening, and how does your soil compare?

The ideal garden soil has at least one spade-depth (and preferably two spade-depths or more) of top soil. The top soil should be (1) free-draining, not prone to waterlogging after heavy rain, (2) easily broken down into a crumbly texture when dug and raked, yet not too sandy and quick to dry out, (3) well-enriched with decayed organic material (from rotted leaves, manure, etc.) and (4) neither very limy nor highly acid, but somewhere between the two (giving a neutral or almost neutral reaction when tested). Do not despair if this sounds nothing like your own soil. The vast majority of gardeners manage quite happily with soils which do not match up to the ideal in one way or another. The four qualities listed above simply give a general indication of what you should be aiming towards, should you be planning to improve a less-than-perfect garden soil in the hope of making it suited to as wide as possible a range of ornamental plants, vegetables and fruits. If your soil falls short of the ideal in any way and if you have, or are planning to have, a vegetable and fruit plot, it is there that you should concentrate your greatest efforts towards achieving 'perfect' soil conditions, as they will make a vast difference to your crops.

In ornamental beds and borders, the wholesale improvement of a difficult soil is the ultimate ideal, but it is not always possible in the short term. It is easier in a really small garden, where the soil areas are not too extensive (and where you really want to get the very best from every inch of ground that you have). But in larger gardens, time and expense may well make instant all-round soil improvement difficult or impossible.

When faced with large areas of a problem soil in ornamental beds and borders, concentrate first and foremost on improving the patch of soil where each new plant is to go in. This gives the young plants a better start in life, so that when their roots later spread out into surrounding unimproved ground, then — having become well established and growing strongly — they will be much better able to cope with any serious problems (such as sticky clay or dry soil). More general border-soil improvement can come later as a long-term process which continues over the years — involving forking in soil-improving materials between plants, annual mulching and lifting any struggling, poorly-growing plants and replanting them in improved soil.

How can you identify soil problems?

A very basic guide to the most difficult soil types, indicating the main problems that you will encounter when gardening on them, is given in the previous chapter. If, from past experience in the garden, you think that you may have a problem soil, you will probably recognize what the difficulties are from the outline given there. In a new garden, lack of experience of what the soil is like in different seasons and weather conditions and of how plants succeed in it may well make closer investigation necessary.

Take a handful of moist soil (if wet, allow it to dry out a little before testing; if dry, dampen it slightly). Gently squeeze and knead the sample in the palm of your hand, forming it into a ball; then try to break the ball gently and crumble the soil through your fingers.

Soil with a high clay content is easily rolled into a smooth, hard ball. It sticks to your hands and is easily moulded into various shapes, like

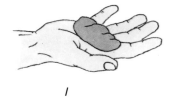

1. Soil with a high clay content.
2. Sandy soil.
3. Good 'loamy' soil.

modelling clay. The soil ball may not be easy to break apart with light pressure, and it will not readily crumble into fine particles.

If the soil is somewhat sticky, but also gritty, forms a ball, but it cannot be moulded like clay, breaks apart easily under light pressure and crumbles well, then it is almost certainly good 'loamy' soil; it has neither too much clay nor too much sand, but a balance of each. A dark colour and traces of decaying plant material (roots, twigs, leaves, etc.) indicate a good content of organic matter.

Very sandy soil will not stick to your hand, will not form a solid ball and will simply run through your fingers. Such soil is commonly low in organic matter, a deficiency which may be indicated by a light colouring.

Be sure to test samples from different beds and borders, as the soil may well vary somewhat from one part of the garden to another (especially in a larger garden).

Check further by general observation and digging. A shallow, chalky soil will be indicated by white chalk fragments in the top-soil or by more or less solid chalk not far below the surface. Stony ground should be obvious, and will indicate that the ground will be free-draining and likely to dry out fairly fast in summer. Peaty soils are not common, but they are easily recognized by anyone who has handled garden peat: spongy and full of semi-decayed plant matter, very dark in colour when wet, poor-drainage and prone to waterlogging.

Is your soil acid or limy?

Shallow, chalky soils are generally very limy, although sometimes a deep soil over chalk may be neutral or acid. Soils in areas of harder limestone bedrock tend to be somewhat less limy, and may vary locally to neutral or even slightly acid. Poorly-drained peaty soils are usually highly acid, as are some sandy soils.

Some ornamental plants and vegetables prefer slightly limy soil. The majority are happiest on neutral soil, though they will tolerate some lime or acidity. Others (notably rhododendrons, azaleas and camellias) will not tolerate lime in the soil, but enjoy slightly acid conditions.

If you are starting a new garden, ask neighbours whether the local soil is acid or limy and look at other gardens in your locality to see which plants

35

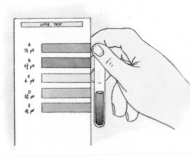

Check soil acidity or lime content with a 'pH' testing-kit, these are inexpensive and easy to use. To do the soil test place a sample of your soil in the tube with indicator fluid, shake a little and then compare the colour with the chart supplied.
A 'pH' reading of 7 is neutral while lower readings indicate acidity and a reading from 7-8 indicates limy soil.

grow well. Thriving rhododendrons indicate a non-limy soil; sickly, yellow-leaved rhododendrons suggest the presence of lime in the soil. Note, however, that your garden soil may vary even from those of next-door neighbours. And the soil may equally vary from one part of your garden to another (particularly in a large garden).

The garden, or parts of it, may over the years have been given regular and heavy doses of manure, compost and acidic nitrate fertilizers. This treatment, which is most likely to have occurred on a long-established vegetable plot, creates highly acid conditions and reduces the liminess of normally limy soils. On the other hand, a garden (or parts of a garden) in an area of naturally acid soil may have been regularly treated with lime to counteract excessive acidity, perhaps making it too limy for rhododendrons and other lime-hating plants. Again, this treatment will most commonly have occurred on vegetable plots.

Soil acidity or lime-content is easily checked with one of the inexpensive 'pH' testing-kits. Simply place a small sample of soil in the tube of indicator fluid, shake, and compare the colour with the chart supplied. A pH reading of about 7 is neutral. Lower readings indicate acidity — from 7 down to 5.5 for soil that is slightly to moderately acid, and below 5.5 for highly acidic soil. A pH reading from 7 to 8 indicates limy soil.

When testing, take care not to handle the soil, as acidic perspiration from your skin can affect the sample and alter the reading; use the tip of a trowel, a clean dry teaspoon, or a knife-blade. Remember, too, to test soil from different parts of the garden, as variations in acidity and liminess may occur even over a relatively small area.

Is your soil short of plant foods?

The three major plant nutrients are nitrogen, phosphates and potassium. All three are essential for healthy growth. Nitrogen encourages fast, leafy growth. Phosphates promote strong root-growth. Potassium is important for free flowering and good fruit production, and also encourages sturdy growth, making plants more resistant to frost and disease.

Very fast-draining soils, such as sandy soils, shallow chalk soils and very stony soils, suffer most from shortages of plant food. Nutrients are quickly washed down into the sub-soil, beyond the reach of most roots, by heavy rain. These soils can become especially short of plant foods after a series of unusually wet seasons. Fertilizers should be applied to the soil during the spring and summer growing season, in smaller doses than is usually recommended and at more frequent intervals, to ensure a constant supply of nutrients (particularly on the vegetable plot). If heavy doses are applied, much of the goodness may wash away before the plants can use it. Avoid applying fertilizers in autumn, as winter rains will tend to wash them out of the soil.

Clay soils are generally fertile and less likely to run quickly short of plant foods; the clay particles attract and hold on to the essential nutrients, preventing them from being readily washed away. The real problem here is to improve the drainage in order to encourage better root-growth. Loamy soils which contain a good balance of clay and sand (and are therefore free-draining, but not nearly as fast-drying as sandy soils) are also far less likely to run out of plant foods over a short period. Soils which are not regularly enriched with organic material (garden compost, leaf mould, well-rotted mature, etc.) tend to run out of plant nutrients much faster than soils where these essential soil-improving materials are regularly dug in or spread as a mulch.

Testing kits and meters are available for measuring the levels of the different plant foods in soil, and they are useful for indicating nutrient shortages. But prevention is always better than cure. The real answer is thoughtful and intelligent use of fertilizers and soil-improving organic materials. Match your applications of these to the needs of the plants, to your soil type and to the weather conditions.

Bear in mind that different types of plant and crops have different nutrient needs. Giving them too much fertilizer of a kind that they do not need in large quantities is wasteful and may even be harmful. Take into account your soil type when deciding how much fertilizer to use and how often to apply it: little and often on fast-draining dry soils, normal doses less frequently on clay and loamy soils; and less altogether if you frequently and generously add compost and manure to the soil. And remember that following an unusually wet season (especially after a series of very wet seasons, one after another) the soil is likely to need more feeding than after dry seasons, particularly if it is fast-draining.

Which fertilizer should you use, and how much?

The range of fertilizers available from shops and garden centres can be bewildering. Some 'compound' fertilizers contain all three essential nutrients. Others provide only one, or sometimes two. And some are specialized fertilizers, containing the full range of nutrients, but with an extra-heavy dose of one or another of them to suit a particular plant type— such as, for example, the 'special' fertilizers for roses, tomatoes and lawns.

COMPOUND FERTILIZERS

Choose a balanced compound fertilizer for general garden use, one that provides roughly equal amounts of all the plant foods, so that none of your plants goes short of essential nutrients. Blood fish and bone fertilizer is an excellent choice for ornamental plants, trees, shrubs and bulbs; and it is equally suitable for vegetables and fruit. This is an organic, balanced general fertilizer which does the soil good (encouraging the proliferation of beneficial soil micro-organisms and promoting a healthy fertile soil) as well as feed your plants. Alternatively, there are balanced chemical fertilizers, which are faster-working than organic feeds and provide a rapid boost to growth in the vegetable garden. But chemical fertilizers do have their drawbacks. They are generally more soluble, and therefore more quickly washed out of the soil and less long-lasting, than organic feeds. They do not feed the natural bacteria which help to keep soil healthy and fertile. And some of them can actually upset the natural balance of useful soil micro-organisms if applied too frequently in heavy doses.

SPECIALIZED FERTILIZERS

Most plants (and lawns) will be reasonably happy on a steady diet of a standard, balanced compound fertilizer. But some do have their preferences and special needs. In particular, check in gardening reference books for the specialized requirements of different vegetables, as a correct feeding routine will make a great different to your crops. In general, as a rough guide, leaf vegetables, such as cabbage and lettuce, need more nitrogen than other crops to encourage fast succulent growth. The root-promoting effect of phosphates is of special benefit to root vegetables, such as carrots, parsnips and potatoes. Potassium, which encourages free-flowering and good fruit-production is particularly important for fruit trees, soft fruits, fruiting vegetables such as tomatoes and cucumbers, and pod-crops (peas and beans).

Fruits and vegetables may be given a specialized feed containing a high dose of the most-needed nutrient, such as a high-potash fertilizer for tomatoes and cucumbers. Or they may be given a 'straight' (single-nutrient) fertilizer, to supplement applications of general compound fertilizer or to correct a soil deficiency. The most commonly used 'straight' chemical fertilizers are sulphate of ammonia (for nitrogen boost), superphosphate (for phosphates) and sulphate of potash (for potassium). The organic alternatives are dried blood (for nitrogen), bonemeal (for phosphates) and bonfire ash (for potassium). The last is stored dry until used.

Beware of giving flowering plants, shrubs and bulbs too much nitrogen, which will promote excessive leafy growth at the expense of flowering. Too much nitrogen will also encourage woody plants (shrubs, trees and climbers) to produce soft growth that is prone to damage from frost and disease. Extra potassium, on the other hand, promotes both free-flowering and tougher growth that is more resistant to frost and disease.

2

LIQUID FERTILIZERS

Choose liquid fertilizers for plants in pots or other containers. Liquid feeds will also give sickly or slow-growing plants a quick boost. And for even more immediate first-aid, the leaves of ailing plants may be sprayed with a foliar fertilizer (which is absorbed straight into the foliage), followed by a liquid or powder feed to the roots to aid longer-term recovery. Never increase fertilizer doses above what is recommended on the pack or bottle. Too much fertilizer will often do more harm than good, and plants are generally better off a little underfed rather than overfed.

3

4

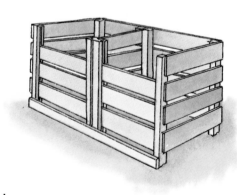

1

This page: Making compost.
1. A two-bay timber compost bin.
2. Use bricks to create air channels under the compost.
3. Add clippings, weeds, kitchen scraps etc. in layers.
4. Water if the heap dries out.
5. Speed up composting with an activator powder.

Facing page: Dianthus deltoides.

5

Has your soil been starved of organic matter?

Remember that organic materials (garden compost, leafmould, well-rotted manure, spent mushroom compost, garden peat, etc.) are as essntial to the health of your soil and plants as fertilizers. They improve the structure of the soil, making heavy soils crumblier, easier to work and better drained. And, of course, they make all soil types less prone to drying out fast during droughts. Plenty of organic matter also encourages (as do organic fertilizers) thriving populations of the vital micro-organisms which keep soil fertile. Without organic material, soils become increasingly dead and lifeless, unable to maintain natural fertility without ever-increasing doses of fertilizer.

The message for gardeners is this: the more compost and other bulky organic materials you put into the ground, the happier your plants will be, and the less money you will need to spend on expensive fertilizers. Do not forget that garden compost is the cheapest soil-improver there is.

Most organic materials, such as garden compost, manures and leaf mould, add some plant nutrients of their own to the soil. Others, such as peat and chopped bark, contain few or no plant foods, and should always have some compound fertilizer mixed with them when added to the soil in large quantities or spread as a thick mulch. Always ensure that compost, manure, and leaf mould are well-rotted before you dig them in.

3

1

1. Viburnum bodnantense. Very popular for its highly scented winter flowers. All viburnums do well on clayey soils.
2. Cornus alba 'Siberica'. Its bright winter shoots are the main attraction. All cornus tolerate heavy clay and wet soils very well.
3. Ajuga 'Burgundy Glow'. Likes moist ground and makes good ground cover in shady corners.
4. Astilbes, hosta and hemerocallis. All good choices for heavy clay soils. Astilbes and hostas also enjoy shade.

2

How do you cope with

problem soils?

CLAY SOILS

Digging in autumn and early winter will help to improve clay soils and make them ready for spring sowing and planting. Leave the ground rough-dug and pile up the clods into ridges so that winter frosts can penetrate them. By spring, repeated freezing and thawing will have crumbled the clay lumps to a finer texture. This is a particularly important practice in the vegetable garden; but it is equally helpful when preparing empty borders for spring planting or a lawn site for spring sowing.

On acid clay soils, spreading lime on bare ground after autumn or winter rough-digging will help to make the clay crumblier still. This is standard practice on acid vegetable plots. But it will make little difference where the soil is already naturally limy and can be positively harmful (check with a pH testing kit).

Take great care not to make your soil too limy, which will do more harm than good. Do not lime the whole of an acid vegetable garden every year, but only about every three years. The best policy is to lime only where the lime-loving brassicas (cabbages, cauliflowers, sprouts, etc.) are to grow, and to move these to a different part of the plot from year to year (which you should do, at any rate, as part of your crop rotation). Beware of liming soil in which plants prefer acid conditions are to be grown; and never lime soil where strongly lime-hating plants such as rhododendrons, azaleas, and camellias are to be planted.

Most important of all for the long-term improvement of a clay soil is to work as much organic matter as possible into the ground — in the form of garden compost, rotted manure, leaf-mould, peat, spent mushroom compost and similar humus-adding materials. These bulky soil-improvers open up the solid-packed structure of the clay, improving drainage. And, as they reach their final stages of decay, the humus they produce (a rich, dark-brown liquid) transforms the nature of the clay, making it much crumblier and easier to work.

To improve the drainage of clay soils further (and more quickly) you can work coarse sand into them, a good way to rapidly improve drainage in smaller garden borders, especially when preparing individual planting sites for new plants and shrubs. For more extensive

4

1. Laburnum watereri 'Vossii'. A smallish tree suitable for smaller gardens. Seen here grown to form a tunnel; a spectacular sight in late spring. Laburnum seeds are poisonous, but this variety sets few seeds so is a safer choice for gardens where children play.
2. Rose 'Ballerina'. All roses do well on clay soils. This variety forms a small bush, flowering all summer long. A good choice for small gardens.
3. Primula denticulata (drumstick primula). The border primulas grow well in damp clayey soils. They prefer some shade so are excellent choices for gloomy corners of the garden.

areas (such as large vegetable plots) the amount of sand required may be prohibitively expensive. Garden centres and local nurseries usually sell suitable sand ready-bagged for just this sort of use. Alternatively, builder's merchants will conveniently deliver ton-loads of loose coarse or sharp sand to your door, and this generally works out cheaper than buying by the bagful.

If very severe waterlogging and surface flooding regularly occurs on heavy clay, you may have to lay land-drains beneath lawns and borders to carry excess water away to a deep stone-filled pit; but this is a job for experts (contact a local landscape gardener for advice). Clay tends to be very fertile once drainage is improved and the texture of the soil made crumblier and most plants and crops will thrive on an improved clay soil. If the clay is particularly heavy, and widescale soil-improvement proves difficult, avoid plants or crops which reference books and catalogues describe as requiring well-drained soil and choose, for the 'backbone' of the garden, plants which will tolerate heavy clay.

Bear in mind that wet clay soils are slower to warm up in spring than lighter, better-drained soils. Therefore Spring sowing and planting should be delayed until the soil is in a suitably dry and warm condition, which will be later than normally recommended in books and seed catalogues.

Take care also to avoid treading on heavy clay soils (or any other soil, for that matter) while the ground is wet. Trampling on wet soil spoils its crumbly structure and reduces its ability to drain freely. When you work on the soil (digging, planting, sowing or whatever), even in dry conditions, it is best to stand on a plank and spread your weight.

DRY SANDY SOILS

The most vital aim with a sandy soil is to improve its water-retaining ability, both to reduce problems arising from summer droughts and to prevent essential plant foods from being quickly washed down below the reach of roots by heavy rains. This is especially important in the vegetable garden.

Loamy top-soil (or even clay soil) bought in by the load and dug into sandy soils will provide an instant answer, but may prove an expensive solution where large areas are involved. The more usual remedy is to get as much bulky organic matter into the soil as you can — garden compost, well-rotted manure, leaf mould, peat and spent mushroom compost. Apart from helping the soil to retain summer moisture, the sticky brown liquid humus that these organic materials produce as they decay will also improve the texture of the soil. It will bind the sandy grains together into larger particles, so that the soil takes on a richer, cake-crumb texture, instead of the dust-dry state that is so typical of very sandy soils.

Do not dig these organic materials too deeply into sandy soil, where they may quickly

4. Leucojum aestivum (summer snowflake). Flowers in late spring (despite the misleading common name) and enjoys both moist soil and some shade.
5. Iris sibirica 'Variegata'. A handsome foliage plant.

6. Hemerocallis 'Burning Daylight'. An exotic day-lily.
7. Cotoneaster 'Cornubia'. The berries last well into winter.

41

disappear. Concentrate them in the top spit (one spade-depth), aiming to build up a layer of richer soil over the sand below. Spreading a layer of compost or similar material over the ground between plants and crops (known as mulching) in late spring or early summer will help to keep the ground moist by reducing water evaporation. But always ensure that the ground is already moist before you mulch and that the mulching material is itself moist; otherwise the mulch will have the opposite effect, absorbing rain and preventing it from reaching the dry soil below.

Shortage of plant foods is a common problem on fast-draining sandy soils, as nutrients are quickly leached away by rain. Apply fertilizers during spring and summer, in smaller and more frequent doses than usually recommended, in order to maintain a constant supply of plant foods during the growing season (especially on vegetable plots and garden areas where fruits are being grown).

Remember that sandy soils are very often acid. If so, adding moisture-retaining humus material will enable the ground to sustain such beautiful lime-hating plants as rhododendrons and azaleas. In the vegetable garden, liming in late winter will be necessary if the soil is strongly acid, since most vegetables prefer neutral or slightly limy growing conditions.

The digging of vegetable plots on sandy soils is best left until spring (shortly before sowing and planting); disturbing and opening up the ground in autumn will increase the danger of winter rains washing plant foods out of the top-soil. Sandy soils warm up and drain fast in spring, so that there should be more opportunity for soil preparation at this time than on a heavier, wetter soil. You may also be able to plant and sow a little earlier than on a heavier soil.

If thorough soil improvement proves difficult (e.g. in a large garden) choose your plants and crops with care. Avoid those described by reference books and catalogues as demanding moist growing conditions. For the backbone of the garden plantings, search out tough, drought-tolerant plants.

SHALLOW, DRY, CHALKY SOILS

Dry chalky soil is treated in much the same way as dry sandy soil, since the basic problems are similar — fast-draining soil prone to drying out rapidly in spring and summer and likely to become short of essential plant foods as these are washed down into the chalk sub-soil by

heavy rains.

Get as much bulky, moisture-retaining organic material (compost, manure, peat, etc.) as possible into the top-soil. Additional top-soil may be spread over the surface to increase the depth of a very shallow soil. And mulching the ground between plants in spring and summer will help to prevent rapid drying.

Avoid deep digging, which will bring up more chalk into the soil. Dig vegetable plots in spring rather than autumn, for the reasons set out in the previous section. And apply fertilizers during spring and summer, in smaller doses and more frequently than normally recommended. Shallow chalk soils are generally very limy and not suitable for lime-hating plants. If you want to grow beautiful lime-haters like rhododendrons, azaleas, and camellias, they should be planted in tubs or raised beds filled with a lime-free, 'ericaceous' potting compost. You may try to make the soil slightly less limy, but on very chalky soils success is likely to be limited. The emphasis in your plant choices should be on drought-resistant plants, avoiding those which require ample summer moisture. On unimproved shallow soil, choose crops for

7

1. Iris danfordiae (yellow flowers) and I. histrioides 'Major' (blue flowers). Most dwarf bulbs enjoy well-drained sandy or chalky soils. And these dwarf 'reticulata' type iris bulbs really need such conditions to grow and flower well.
2. Oenothera missouriensis. A low-spreading evening primrose species which flowers non-stop throughout summer.
3. Kniphofia variety. Popular summer flowering border plants.
4. Helianthemum nummularium 'The Bride' (rock rose). The rock roses are very useful low-spreading shrubby plants flowering non-stop during summer. Other varieties are available in yellow, orange, pink and red.
5. Cistus 'Silver Pink' (sun rose). The sun roses like well drained soil conditions and also benefit from a sheltered site to reduce winter frost damage.
6. Agapanthus 'Headbourne hybrids' (blue African lily).
7. Eschscholtzia californica (Californian poppy). Annual.
8. Mesembryanthemum (Livingstone daisy). Needs a hot sunny site to flower freely.

8

the vegetable garden carefully, those which demand plenty of water may disappoint you, and root vegetables may be a problem. Choose short-rooted varieties of carrot and parsnip.

PEATY SOILS

Peaty soils are the very opposite to chalky soils: poor-draining, prone to waterlogging and highly acid. When drained, they can be very suitable for lime-hating shrubs like rhododendrons and for natural peat-lovers like the heathers. For most other plants and crops, liming to reduce acidity is generally essential. Laying land-drains is often necessary where waterlogging problems are severe (seek professional advice). Digging in coarse sand will help if only small areas of ground are involved; larger areas will need a great deal of sand. Working loamy top-soil into the peat will also greatly impove it. Peaty soils are likely to be short of at least some plant foods, and therefore they may need quite heavy doses of fertilizer when first cultivated.

STONY SOILS

Remove any large stones which appear on the surface or are brought up by digging. Do not worry about smaller stones, as these aid soil drainage. If the ground tends to dry out fast in spring and summer, add moisture-retaining organic material as recommended for dry,

1

2

3

4

6

7

8

5

sandy and chalky soils. Mulching between plants will also help to keep the soil moist. In the vegetable garden, root crops may be disappointing; choose short-rooted varieties of carrot and parsnip.

1. Alstroemeria 'Ligtu hybrids' (Peruvian lily). Exotic summer flowering lily-like plants for hot sunny borders.

2. Lavandula 'Hidcote'. One of the best lavender varieties.

3. Helianthemum 'Rhodanthe Carneum' (rock rose). Easy rock plants, the helianthemums are also good for evergreen ground cover on dry soils.

4. Hypericum patulum 'Hidcote'. A very useful shrub, flowering

non-stop all summer long.

5. Pulsatilla vulgaris (pasque flower). A charming spring flowering rock plant.

6. Dianthus deltoides (maiden pink). An easy rock plant, and good for dry borders and banks.

7. Cistus 'Sunset' (sun rose).

8. Kolkwitzia amabilis (beauty bush). Flowers late spring.

ACID SOILS

Acidity is not necessarily a great problem, unless it is excessive (check with a pH testing kit, available from garden shops). Acid soils particularly suit lime-hating plants and shrubs like rhododendrons. Do not lime the soil where these are to be planted.

For most other plants, some liming will be beneficial if the acidity is excessive. This is particularly important for vegetable crops, some of which do better on neutral or slightly limy soil; the most notable exception is the potato, which is less apt to scab on acid soils and should not go into recently limed ground. The best time to lime is after autumn or winter digging. But take care not to lime at the same time as (or shortly before or after) digging in manure or spreading fertilizer; the lime may react to them and destroy some of their important plant nutrients.

Be careful not to over-lime, since doing so can cause as much trouble as excess acidity. On a vegetable plot, the best method is to lime the ground where brassicas (cabbages, sprouts, cauliflowers, etc.) are to go each year; so that as these rotate around the plot from year to year (which they ought to do) the whole area is gradually limed every three to four years.

LIMY SOILS

Lime is not really a problem, unless you have to cope with an excessively limy and dry, shallow soil which lies over chalk (for which, *see* the recommendations above for shallow, dry chalky soils).

A moderately limy (non-chalky) garden soil will sustain most plants, fruits and vegetables quite successfully. However, lime-hating plants such as rhododendrons will not thrive unless you can reduce the liminess of the soil to neutral or slighty acid. These may, however, be grown in containers or raised beds, in a non-limy 'ericaceous' potting compost (or a home-made mixture of peat, sand and fertilizer). If in doubt about whether or to what extent your soil is limy, check it with a pH testing kit.

Small areas of soil may be made less limy by the addition of large quantities of peat and by working in flowers of sulphur (available from garden shops). The chemical nitrogen fertilizer, sulphate of ammonia, will also make soil more acid, but in large doses this can kill essential soil micro-organisms and upset the soil's natural balance; so be wary. If the soil's lime content is naturally low, these measures may make it possible for some lime-hating plants (such as

1

2

rhododendrons and the summer-flowering heathers) to survive (but they will not thrive as well as they would on naturally acid soils). Even when you do manage to make patches of limy soil less so, the lime will generally creep back eventually, from the surrounding soil. Lime-hating plants may then require some help to keep them going.

The most obvious sign of distress from lime-hating plants struggling to grow in limy ground is a yellowing of the leaves (technically known as chlorosis). The yellowing is caused by a shortage of iron and magnesium, essential minerals which lime-hating plants find it

difficult to get in large enough quantities from limy soil. Garden shops sell 'sequestered' iron and magnesium tonics which (when watered around distressed lime-hating plants) will help to correct the deficiency.

In a limy vegetable garden, planting potatoes with lashings of compost will help to keep the crop free from scab disease (which is always worst on limy ground). Most other vegetables are happy with moderately limy soil, but regular and heavy doses of compost (which slightly increases acidity) are recommended for very limy soil.

3

1. Dwarf evergreen Azaleas 'Hinodegiri' (red flowers) and 'Hinomayo' (pink). All azaleas and rhododendrons must have non-limy soil.
2. Camellia williamsii variety 'Donation'. The camellias are another important group of lime hating shrubs.
3. A mature heather garden. Most summer-flowering heathers (e.g. Calluna vulgaris and Erica cinerea varieties) need non-limy soil. The summer flowering Erica vagans varieties will tolerate slightly limy soil. Winter flowering heathers (Erica carnea and E. darleyensis varieties) do not mind lime in the soil.

Some plants will not grow in limy or chalky soils. They must have neutral or acid soil, or be grown in tubs or pots of non-limy 'ericaceos' potting compost.

47

PLANTS FOR PURPOSES

Thoughtful plant selection is a vital part of successful gardening, essential if you wish to avoid making some of the most common gardening mistakes and creating future problems for yourself. The lists on the following pages aim to help you to solve the puzzle of choosing plants to meet different requirements and to suit different situations. In order to offer as wide a choice as possible, descriptive notes, particularly in the more general lists, are not always given (and where they do appear, they have been kept very brief). Once you have a plant's name, full descriptions may easily be looked up in reference books and catalogues. The intention here is to point you in the right direction, so that you know what to look for when seeking suitable choices for different purposes and sites.

How do you ensure plenty of 'permanent' colour and interest in the garden year after year?

It is the permanent trees, shrubs, climber and perennial border plants which make up the backbone of the garden, providing colour and interest in all seasons and, over the years, gradually developing to build up an increasingly mature and pleasing outlook. Too few of these permanent subjects in the planting scheme, and too heavy a reliance on plants for instant but temporary displays, will result in a garden which never really matures, a garden which remains basically an unchanging display area for setting out spring and summer bedding plants — with a lot of bare earth to stare at during winter.

When planning permanent plantings, always bear in mind the prime rules of good planting design. Ensure that there is plenty of variation in height and scale within your plant groupings; aim for a good balance between evergreen and deciduous shrubs; and try to arrange for some colour and interest in all four seasons, not just in spring and summer.

You cannot beat trees for lending a garden that desirable mature look and for creating the greatest possible variations of height and scale in the garden layout. Without at least one, a garden will tend to look flat and lifeless. Even where space is strictly limited, try to find room for at least one small tree.

Evergreens are essential, both for year-round screening and for winter foliage. But do not go overboard with them. Remember that deciduous shrubs are equally valuable and help to create an ever-changing outlook from season to season, with their fresh spring leaves, darker summer foliage, autumn leaf tints, and (often handsome) bare winter stems — not to mention their flowers for different seasons.

Unfortunately there are few reliably hardy evergreen climbers (with the notable exception of the ivies); the vast majority are deciduous. If you want a year-round evergreen climbing screen or wall-covering, consider an evergreen wall shrub.

Hardy perennial border plants are equally indispensable for permanent planting schemes. Most flower in spring and summer, just when you want to have your brightest garden display, while some provide welcome colour during the colder months of the year.

The great majority of hardy perennials are herbaceous plants (dying down for the winter). A few, however, are evergreen or semi-evergreen, thus helping to clothe the ground with some foliage during the winter. These include: *Achillea 'Moonshine'; bergenia; Campanula persicifolia; dianthus* (garden pinks); *Euphorbia wulfenii; helleborus* (Christmas rose, Lenten rose, and various handsome, green-flowered species); *Iris foetidissima; Phormium tenax* (slightly tender, recommended for sheltered southern gardens only); *Stachys lanata* (woody silver leaves); *Tellima grandiflora 'Purpurea'* (purple leaves).

Bulbs are the other mainstay for permanent plantings. Most may be left in the ground to grow into larger clumps year by year (although some are also commonly used for temporary spring bedding displays, being lifted after flowering, to make way for summer bedding plants). Remember that bulbs are not for spring colour alone; there are many which flower in summer and autumn, and even some in winter. Bear in mind also that a few of the summer-flowering bulbs (notably the gladioli) are not hardy and must be lifted in autumn and stored frost-free over winter.

Which plants will provide

winter colour?

Trees and shrubs:

chimonanthus (scented yellow flowers); conifers (golden-foliage varieties such as the slow-growing *Thuja occidentalis 'Rheingold'*, one of the very best); *Cornus alba* (red shoots); *Daphne mezereum* (perfumed purple flowers); *Elaeagnus pungens 'Maculata'* (golden-centred evergreen leaves); *Erica carnea* and *E. darleyensis* (winter-flowering heather varieties, including some with golden winter foliage); *Garrya elliptica* (long, drooping grey catkins, evergreen); *Hamamellis mollis* (fragrant yellow flowers); *Ilex altaclarensis 'Golden King'* (the best golden-leaved holly); *Jasminum nudiflorum* (yellow flowers); *mahonia* (yellow flowers, evergreen); *Prunus subhirtella 'Autumnalis Rosea'* (pink autumn - and winter-flowering cherry); *pyracantha* (red or orange berries, evergreen); *Senecia greyii* (silver-grey evergreen leaves); *Skimmia reevesiana* (red berries, evergreen); *Viburnun bodnantense* (fragrant pink flowers); *Viburnum tinus* (pink and white flowers, evergreen).

Bulbs

(all dwarf-growing types):

Cyclamen coum (ruby-red or pink flowers, leaves often silver-splashed); *Eranthis hyemalis* (yellow buttercup-flowers); *Galanthus nivalis* (common snowdrop; single and double flowered types available) and *G. elwesii* (giant Turkish snowdrop; larger flowered); *Iris histiroides 'Major'* (sky-blue flowers), *I. danfordiae* (yellow flowers) and *I. reticulata* varieties (shades of blue or purple).

Careful selection of perennial plants, bulbs and shrubs will ensure colour and interest in the garden all year round. Be sure to include plants for autumn and winter colour in your schemes.

Previous page:
1. Colchicum speciosum. The colchicums (often incorrectly called 'autumn crocus') are invaluable for a splash of brilliant autumn colour.
2. Helleborus orientalis (the Lenten rose). Flowers from late winter to early spring.

2

3

4

*1. Eranthis hyemalis (winter aconite).
Good for naturalizing.
2. Iris histrioides 'Major'. One of the best dwarf
'reticulata' bulb irises. Flowers Jan-Feb.
3. Iris unguicularis. Blooms throughout winter.
Scented.
4. Hamamelis mollis 'Goldcrest' (witch hazel).
Sweetly scented.
5. Viburnum bodnantense. Strongly perfumed
flowers, good in vases.*

5

What are the best choices for autumn colour?

Shrubs and climbers (for bright autumn leaf colour): *Acer japonicum* and *A. palmatum* varieties (slow-growing Japanese maples); *amelanchier; azalea* (deciduous types); *Cotoneaster horizontalis* (plus red berries); *enkianthus; hamamelis; parthenocissus* (Virginia creeper, Boston ivy, etc.); *Rhus typhina* (stag's horn sumach); *Rosa rugosa* (plus large red hips); *Vitis vinifera 'Brant'* and *V. coignetiae* (ornamental vines).

Trees and shrubs (with bright autumn fruits and berries): *cotoneaster* (all types); *crataegus* (ornamental thorns); *malus* (ornamental crab apples); *pyracantha* (firethorns); *shrub roses* (the best are *Rosa moyesii* and *R. rugosa); sorbus* (Mountain ash varieties); *stranvaesia; Viburnum opulus.*

Perennial plants and bulbs (for autumn flowers): *Anemone japonica* (pink and white varieties); *aster* (the popular Michaelmas daisies); *cimicifuga* (tall white spikes); *colchicum* (large lilac-pink, purple-pink or white goblet-flowers, commonly but wrongly called 'Autumn crocus'); *Crocus speciosus* (large lilac-blue flowers, the best of the true autumn crocus; others are available in some bulb catalogues); *Cyclamen hederifolium* (dainty pink or white flowers and silver-marbled leaves, also sold as *C. neapolitanum*); *Nerine bowdenii* (glistening pink trumpets, for a sheltered sunny spot); *schizostylis* (spikes of red or pink flowers depending on the variety).

I. Acer palmatum 'Osakazuki' (Japanese maple). Few other trees and shrubs can rival the Japanese maples for fiery red, orange and yellow autumn leaf colours. Most Acer palmatum and A. japonicum varieties are good choices. All are ideal for small gardens, being either slow-growing shrubs or small trees. Look out also for A. griseum (the paperbark maple). The autumn leaf tints are as good as its Japanese cousins, and the peeling red-brown bark is handsome all year. This is also a slow-growing small tree ideal for restricted spaces.

2

4

5

3

2. *Schizostylis coccinea 'Major'.* Flowering Sept-Nov, schizostylis need well-drained soil but regular watering in dry weather to do well. The pink varieties *'Mrs Hegarty'* and *'Viscountess Byng'* are also worth seeking out.
3. *Crocus speciosus* (true autumn crocus). Not to be confused with the false 'autumn crocus', the colchicums (see pages 48 and 50). Others to look out for include *Crocus medius* (lilac-purple) and *C. kotschyanus* (alias *C. zonatus*; pale lilac).
4. *Nerine bowdenii.* The only reliably hardy nerine. It flowers most freely in a hot sunny bed at the base of a south or west wall.
5. *Colchicum hybrid 'Waterlily'.*

Which plants produce 'instant' displays?

These are the types of plants widely used in garden bedding displays, hanging baskets, window boxes and tubs to provide a mass of colour in spring and summer. Many are also useful for providing extra summer colour among the permanent shrubs and perennial plants in mixed borders (especially while the garden is young and there are plenty of gaps between the permanent plants).

The popular fast-growing annuals are strictly temporary plants, dying in autumn after a single summer's colourful flowering display; they must be replaced with new plants each year, but are inexpensive to raise from seed. The tender summer-flowering perennial bedding plants must be lifted in autumn and kept safe from freezing over during winter, planted or stored in pots or boxes of peat. Before filling the garden with these plants, bear in mind the comments made at the beginning of the previous section about permanent plants *versus* temporary plants.

Hardy annuals are easily raised during spring in a cold-frame or unheated greenhouse, or they may be sown directly into the garden soil where they are to flower. Half-hardy annuals are less simple and must be raised in warmth, either under glasss or on a sunny windowsill indoors; many gardeners prefer to buy ready-grown plants in late spring from garden centres, nurseries and shops. Detailed sowing instructions are usually given on seed packets.

It is important to remember that half-hardy annuals should not be planted out in spring until the danger of sharp late frost is past. All annuals raised under glass or indoors should also be fully 'hardened off' before planting out in the garden.

Hardy annuals, half-hardy annuals, and tender perennials provide colour during summer. But for spring bedding, the gardener uses a mixture of bulbs, early-flowering hardy perennials (such as primroses) and biennial plants. The biennials are short-lived plants similar to annuals, but are sown in early summer and planted out in autumn, to flower the following spring (after which they are discarded).

If bulbs and hardy perennials are used for spring bedding and must be dug up after flowering to make way for summer bedding plants, take care to treat these more permanent, longer-lived plants correctly after lifting. Bulbs whose leaves have not died down by lifting time should be replanted in a sunny corner, or in pots, to finish their growing cycle. Do not dry the bulbs off for summer storage until the leaves have turned completely yellow. Primroses and polyanthus should be immediately replanted in a shady or semi-shady place, kept fed and watered regularly during the summer, and lifted in autumn for dividing-up and replanting if required again for spring bedding.

Remember to aim for a variety of plant heights in bedding schemes. A bed of plants all about the same height will make for a flat and therefore rather boring feature.

What plants make good spring bedding displays?

Plants:

perennial primroses and *polyanthus;* biennial pansies, wallflowers, Bellis perennis varieties (ornamental daisies), and *myosotis* (forget-me-nots).

Bulbs:

daffodils (dwarf-growing 'rockery' varieties are excellent for bedding, in addition to the larger types); tulips (good dwarf varieties available here, too, as well as the taller hybrids); hyacinths; large-flowered Dutch crocus varieties; and scillas.

Which seasonal bedding plants make good summer flowers?

Hardy annuals:

Alyssum maritimum (sweet alyssum); *calendula* (pot marigold); *centaurea* (cornflour); *dimorphotheca* (star of the Veldt); *eschscholtzia* (Californian poppy); *godetia; gypsophila* (baby's breath); *helianthus* (sunflower); *helichrysum* (straw flower, good for dried flower arrangements); *iberis* (candytuft); *Lavatera trimestris* (mallow); *limnanthes* (poached egg plant); *malcolmia* (Virginia stock); *nemophila* (baby blue eyes); *nigella* (love in a mist); *Papaver rhoeas* (poppies); *Tropaeolum majus* (nasturtium); *viscaria.*

Half-hardy annuals:

agertum (floss flower); *amaranthus* (love lies bleeding); *antirrhinum* (snapdragon); *Begonia semperflorens* (fibrous-rooted begonia); *calceolaria* (slipper flower); *cosmos* (cosmea);

2

3

1. Impatiens (busy Lizzie). Half-hardy annual. Flowers well either in sun or shade.
2. Tulipa praestans 'Fusilier'. Superb dwarf tulip for bedding displays, tubs and windowboxes.
3. Polyanthus. An easy hardy perennial for spring displays.
4. Myosotis alpestris (forget-me-not). Does well in shade.
5. Lobelia (pale blue flowered variety). A popular low-growing or trailing annual used for bedding, tubs, windowboxes and hanging baskets.

4

5

dahlia (bedding dahlias); *gazania; heliotropium* (heliotrope, or cherry pie); *impatiens* (busy Lizzie); *Limonium sinuatum* (statice, a good 'everlasting' for dried flower arrangements); *lobelia; mesembryanthemum* (Livingstone daisy); *mimulus* (monkey flower); *nemesia; nicotiana* (ornamental flowering tobbaco plant); *petunia; phlox* (annual phlox); *Salvia splendens; tagetes* (African marigold, French marigold); *verbena; zinnia.*

Annual climbing plants (summer flowering; grown quickly from seed):
ipomoea (morning glory; half-hardy annual); *lathyrus* (sweet pea; hardy annual; the 'old fashioned' mixtures now widely available are the most sweetly-scented, smaller-flowered, but truly lovely); *Thunbergia alata* (black-eyed Susan; half-hardy annual); *tropaeolum* (climbing nasturtiums; hardy annual).

Tender perennials (for summer colour, needing to be lifted in autumn and kept frost-free over winter):
begonia (tuberous begonias); *fuchsia* (bedding fuchsias); *pelargonium* (more commonly known, incorrectly, as zonal and ivy-leaved geraniums; the true geraniums are hardy border plants).

Tender summer-flowering bulbs (lift in autumn and store frost-free over winter):
freesea ('treated' corms, planted in late spring); *gladiolus* (both tall-stemmed varieties and the smaller and more elegant 'Nanus' varieties); *ixia* (South African corn lily); *sparaxis* (harlequin flower); *tigridia* (tiger flower).

Silver foliage plants (for leaf contrasts among summer bedding):
Senecio cineraria 'Silver Dust', also known as *S. maritima 'Silver Dust'* (ferny leaves; half-hardy annual); *Helichrysum petiolatum* (trailing stems and round leaves; tender perennial).

1

2

3

4

What are the fastest-growing plants for quick garden hedging, screening wind-shelter?

Evergreen hedges:
Berberis stenophylla (golden spring flowers); *Cotoneaster simonsii* (semi-evergreen, red berries); *Cupressocyparis leylandii* (Leyland cypress; the very fastest-growing evergreen hedging plant, up to 3ft a year when established); *ligustrum* (privet; the usual green type, and also a slower-growing golden variety for smaller hedges); *Prunus laurocerasus* (laurel; stands dry shade well, so good for hedging between and beneath large trees); *pyracantha* (red or orange winter berries); *Thuja plicata* (fast growing conifer, tolerates shallow chalk soil well).

Deciduous hedges:
forsythia (yellow spring flowers); *Crataegus monogyna* (hawthorn, quickthorn); *Philadelphus 'Virginal'* (double-flowered fragrant mock-orange); large shrub roses, e.g. *Rose 'Zephirine Drouhin'* (scented, double pink, thornless), *Rose 'Nevada'* (single cream-white flowers, almost thornless), *Rose 'Marguerite Hilling* (single rose-pink) and *Rosa rubrifolia* (purple-grey leaves), all quickly growing to 6-7ft in height; *Lombardy poplar* (very fast-growing, but should not be planted closer than 60ft to buildings or drains, so only for large gardens).

1. Begonia semperflorens (fibrous rooted begonia). A popular summer bedding plant. It thrives best in moist soil with some shade, so is a good choice for those gloomier garden beds and borders, and for window boxes and hanging baskets on shady walls.
2. Pyracantha variety 'Orange Glow' (firethorn). Pyracanthas are easy and fast-growing evergreen shrubs for quick year-round coverage of walls and fences.
3. Yew hedges are slow growing but extremely handsome.
4. Box is a good choice if you want a neat low-growing hedge.

57

Which are the fast-growing shrubs for quick screening?

Some of the fast-growing hedging plants recommended (the more ornamental ones) may also be used as single specimens or in groups, to screen unsightly features, or in mixed shrub plantings along garden boundaries to provide fast informal shelter and privacy.

Other fast-growing (flowering) shrubs well suited to these purposes include the following: *buddleia; Cytisus scoparius* (common broom); *Cotoneaster 'Cornubia'* (evergreen, red berries); *syringa* (lilac); *ribes* (flowering currant); *Stranvaesia davidiana* (semi-evergreen, red berries); *Viburnum bodnantense* (fragant pink winter flowers).

Which plants make neater and more manageable hedges?

Evergreen hedges:
Berberis darwinii (small glossy leaves, golden spring flowers); *Buxus sempervirens* (box hedge; will tolerate shade); *Escallonia ingramii* (pink summer flowers; not for cold exposed sites, but a good seaside hedge); *Lonicera nitida* (very neat, with small box-like leaves; stands shade well); golden privet (slower and neater than the green privet, needs less clipping); *Taxus baccata* (yew; a superb slow-growing hedge of darkest green; very classy choice); *Viburnum tinus* (pink and white winter flowers).

Deciduous hedges:
beech (slow-growing, and a good all-year screen, retaining its handsome russet-coloured autumn leaves throughout winter when clipped into a hedge; tolerates chalky soils); hornbeam (similar to beech, but a better choice for heavy clay soils); *Prunus cistena* (white spring flowers, bright crimson-red young leaves); *Rosa rugosa* (crimson, pink or white perfumed flowers all summer, followed by large red hips).

1

2

What are the fastest-growing climbers and wall-shrubs for disguising ugly buildings, walls and fences?

Evergreens:

Lonicera japonica 'Halliana' (semi-evergreen, cream-flowered, fragrant honeysuckle); *pyracantha* (glossy evergreen leaves, red or orange winter berries)

Deciduous:

Clematis montana varieties (white or pink spring flowers); *Hydrangea petiolaris* (climbing hydrangea, white summer flowers); *parthenocissus* (Virginia creeper); *Polygonum baldschuanicum* (Russian vine, pinky-white flowers in summer and autumn); *Rosa filipes 'Kifsgate'* (may grow 10ft or more a year; clusters of fragrant, single white rose flowers); *Vitis coignetiae* (ornamental vine, brilliant autumn leaf tints).

3

5

I. Cupressocyparis leylandii (the Leyland cypress). One of the very fastest growing hedges (3-4ft a year when established).
2. Berberis darwinii. A handsome evergreen flowering shrub which makes a small hedge.
3. Polygonum baldschuanicum (the Russian vine). An extremely fast growing climber (6ft or more a year). Needs plenty of space.
4. Lavatera olbia 'Rosea' (shrub mallow). Very fast growing shrub (5-6ft in one season).
5. Clematis montana 'Rubens'. A vigorous spring-flowered climber for covering large areas.

4

59

1. Green beech hedge showing autumn leaf colour. The leaves hang on throughout winter.
2. Escallonia macrantha (green foliage) and Griselinia littoralis (yellow-green leaves). Both makes good coastal hedges.
3. Hydrangea petiolaris (climbing hydrangea). A fast growing self-clinging climber for either sunny or shady walls.
4. Ribes sanguineum (flowering currant). A popular fast-growing shrub frequently used for hedging and fast screening.

60

What to choose for labour-saving ground cover?

Low-growing, spreading ground cover plants are useful for reducing garden maintenance, their thick foliage smothering weed seedlings and helping to keep weeding chores to the minimum. They are also handy for covering up areas of bare soil in difficult situations such as steep banks and patches of dry shade, for hiding unsightly features such as manhole covers, and for softening, with their spreading foliage, the hard straight edges of large areas of paving for concrete.

Take care to kill or dig out perennial weed roots before planting ground-cover, particularly the more stubborn and deep-rooting weeds such as dock, dandelion, couch grass and bindweed. These may prove difficult to get rid of if their roots are left in the ground to sprout up through established ground-cover. When covering large areas of ground, groups of three or more plants of the same variety together will produce the boldest visual effects.

Low-growing evergreens provide the most effective year-round ground cover. But spreading deciduous shrubs and herbaceous plants can be almost as useful. They cover the soil with foliage and flowers in spring and summer, helping to keep down weeds and (in the case of deciduous shrubs) providing some cover with their twiggy growth in winter.

Evergreen ground-cover shrubs:

Cotoneaster 'Coral Beauty', *C. microphyllus*, *C. 'Skogholm'* (red autumn berries, tolerate shade); *calluna* and *erica* (summer and winter flowering heathers); *Euonymus fortunei* varieties (variegated foliage, tolerate shade); *hedera* (ivies, tolerate dry shade); *helianthemum* (summer-flowering rock rose); *Hypericum calycinum* (yellow summer flowers, tolerates dry shade, but invasive); *juniperus* (low-spreading junipers, notably the fast-growing *Juniperus horizontalis* varieties, shade tolerant); *Mahonia aquifolium* (holly-like leaves, yellow winter flowers, stands dry shade); *vinca* (periwinkles, blue spring flowers, tolerate dry shade, but invasive).

Deciduous ground-cover shrubs:

Cornus canadensis (white summer flowers, will stand some shade); *Cotoneaster horizontalis* (red berries, autumn leaf colour, stands shade); *Cytisus kewensis* (cream-flowered spreading broom); *potentilla* (masses of white, yellow or orange-red flowers throughout summer, will tolerate dry shade, but flowers best in sun); low-spreading *shrub roses* (e.g. the varieties 'Max Graf', 'Swany' and 'Red Blanket'). Remember that you want ground cover plants to establish and spread as fast as possible. Prepare the ground well, working in peat or compost plus compound fertiliser.

Perennial border plants for ground-cover:

Achillea 'Moonshine' (silvery foliage all year); *Ajuga reptans* varieties (colourful foliage, best in shade); *aubrietia* (good on poor dry soil); *bergenia* (evergreen leaves, tolerates dry shade); *Geranium 'Johnson's Blue'* and *G. 'Wargrave Pink'*; *Hellebrous orientalis* (Lenten rose, shade tolerant); *hosta* (best in shade, not for very dry soils); *Lamium maculatum 'Beacon Silver'* (silvery leaves, stands shade); *Saxifraga umbrosa* (London pride, good in shade); *sedum* (stonecrops, good for very dry sunny areas); *Stachys lanata* (large silvery felted leaves all year round); *thymus* (ornamental thymes); *veronica*.

5

6

7

5. *Hypericum calycinum* (rose of Sharon). Good evergreen ground cover for very dry and shady places, such as under trees and large shrubs or in the dry soil at the base of a large hedge. Very invasive (by underground runners) and can become a pest.

6. Heathers also make excellent evergreen ground cover. Include golden-leaved ones for variety and winter foliage colour. Work peat into the planting site.

7. *Vinca Minor* (lesser periwinkle). Evergreen and fast spreading by trailing stems. Suitable for dry and shady areas.

61

PLANTS
FOR
SITUATIONS

Which are the best plants for

difficult shady situations?

Reasonably moist, shady borders are not
difficult to cope with, as many beautiful shade-
loving plants will thrive there. More difficult
are areas of dry shade, such as under large trees
or on the shady side of a tall hedge. In the
following lists '(Dry)' following plant names
indicates the better choices for such situations.
These plants will grow equally well (and usually
better) in not-so-dry shade. Evergreen varieties
in the following lists are marked '(E)'.

Shrubs:

Acer palmatum, A. Japonicum (Japanese
maples); *arundinaria* (bamboos) (E); *aucuba*
(E); *azalea* (evergreen and deciduous types);
buxus (box) (E) (Dry); *camellia* (E); *choisya* (E);
Cornus canadensis (creeping dogwood);
cotoneaster (evergreen and deciduous varieties)
(Dry); *Euonymus fortunei* varieties (E) (Dry);
hedera (ivies) (E) (good evergreen ground-
cover); *hydrangea; Hypericum calycinum* (E)
(Dry) (strong ground-cover): *ilex* (hollies) (E)
(Dry); *juniperus* (spreading junipers); *ligustrum*
(privet) (Dry); *mahonia* (E) (Dry); *philadelphus;
potentilla* (Dry); *Prunus laurocerasus* (E) (Dry)
(cherry laurel), *P. lusitanica* (E) (Dry) (Portugal
laurel); *pyracantha* (E); *rhododendron* (E), *rubus*
(ornamental brambles) (Dry); *Sambuscu racemos
'Plumsoa Aurea'* (goldern fern-leaved elder);
sarcococca (E) (Dry); *skimmia* (E) (Dry);
stranvaesia (semi-E); *taxus* (E) (yew) (Dry);
viburnum (evergreen and deciduous types) (Dry).

1. Pyracantha 'Orange Glow'.
2. Hosta fortunei.
*3. Cotoneaster horizontalis (in berry) and
Japanese maple.*
4. Hedera colchica 'Dentata Variegata'.

3

2

4

Border plants:

Alchemilla mollis (Dry); *Ajuga reptans; Anemone japonica* (Dry); *aquilegia* (columbine); *astilbe; bergenia* (Dry); *Campanula persicifolia, C. latifolia* (bellflowers); *cimicifuga; convallaria* (lily of the valley); *dicentra* (bleeding heart); *dodecatheon* (shooting stars); *epimedium* (Dry); *Euphorbia robbiae* (Dry); *ferns* (most will tolerate dry shade); *Gentiana asclepiadea* (willow gentian); *Geranium 'Johnson's Blue'; helleborus* (Christmas rose, Lenten rose, and various handsome yellow-green flowered species) (Dry); *hosta; Iris foetidissima* (Dry); *lamium* (ornamental dead nettles) (Dry); *Meconopsis cambrica* (Welsh poppy) (Dry); *Meconopsis betonicifolia, M. grandis* (blue Himalayan poppies); *polygonatum* (Solomon's seal) (Dry); *primula* (border primulas); primroses; polyanthus; *pulmonaria* (Dry); *Saxifraga umbrosa* (London pride); *tellima; vinca* (periwinkle); *viola* (violets).

Bulbs, corms and tubers:

Anemone nemorosa (wind anemone) (Dry); *cyclamen* (hardy species) (Dry); *eranthis* (winter aconite) (Dry); *erythronium* (dog's tooth violet, and American trout lilies); *galanthus* (snowdrops); *leucojum* (snowflakes); *Lilium martagon* (turk's cap lily).

Bedding plants:

Begonia semperflorens; calceolaria; fuchsia; impatiens (busy Lizzie); *lobelia; myosotis* (forget-me-not); *pansy; primrose; polyanthus.*

Climbers and wall-shrubs:

Camellia (E); *chaenomeles* (ornamental quince); *Clematis jackmanii* hybrids (e.g. 'Nelly Moser'); *Cotoneaster horizontalis; Euonymus fortunei* varieties (E); *hedera* (ivies) (E); *Hydrangea petiolaris; Jasminum nudiflorum* (winter jasmine); *Lonicera japonica* (Japanese honeysuckle) (semi-E); *parthenocissus* (Virginia creeper, Boston ivy); *Polygonum baldschuanicum* (Russian vine); *pyracantha (E); rubus* (ornamental brambles).

1

2

3

4

5

Plants for shady situations.

1. Meconopsis cambrica (Welsh poppy). A charming little plant which seeds itself freely about.

2. Polypodium vulgare (common polypody). A handsome evergreen fern for moist or dry shade.

3. Chaenomeles 'Pink Lady'. A variety of the popular 'japonica' or ornamental quince. Good on walls, either sunny or shady.

4. Primula 'Wanda'. A dainty and very free-flowering primrose.

5. Anemone nemorosa 'Allenii'. A blue form of the wood anemone.

6. Choisya ternata (Mexican orange blossom). Sweetly scented flowers are produced from late spring to early summer.

7. Helleborus niger (Christmas rose). Flowering Jan-March, the flowers are best protected with a cloche or pane of glass.

8. Galanthus nivalis (common snowdrop). Good for naturalizing.

9. Helleborus orintalis (Lenten rose). Flowers in late winter.

10. Primula denticulata (the drumstick primula).

65

1

2

3

Plants for clay soils:

1. Leucojum aestivum (summer snowflake). Prefers moist soil and will stand shade, although it does flower best in sun. Actually flowers in late spring, despite the misleading common name.

2. Hemerocallis variety 'Golden Orchid' (daylily) and border phlox appreciate plenty of peat or compost in the soil and may need heavy watering in droughts.

3. Primula vulgaris (the wild primrose). Superb in borders or for naturalizing. Good in shade. Never dig up plants from the wild. Nursery-grown plants are widely available and primroses are easily raised from seed.

4. Iris sibirica. Best in moist sites but it does well in ordinary garden borders if watered in dry weather.

5. Astilbes. Prefer moist soil.

Which plants are particularly good choices for clay soils?

TREES, SHRUBS AND CONIFERS

arundinaria (bamboos); berberis; betula (birch); chaenomeles (quince); cahaecyparis (cypresses); choisya (Mexican orange blossom); carpinus (hornbeam); cornus (dogwoods); cotoneaster; crataegus (ornamental thorns); cytisus (brooms); deutzia; escallonia; forsythia; hypericum; ilex (hollies); juniperus (junipers); laburnum; malus (crab-apples); mahonia; magnolia; metasequoia (dawn redwood); philadelphus (mock-orange); pinus (pines); potentilla; prunus (flowering cherries and laurels); pyracantha; ribes (flowering currant); roses (all types grow well on clay soils); salix (willows); sorbus (mountain ash); taxus (yew); thuja; viburnum; weigela.

CLIMBERS

hedera (ivies); Polygonum baldschuanicum; climbing and rambling roses.

BORDER PLANTS:

Ajuga reptans; Astilbe; astrantia; Campanula lactiflora, C. persicifolia; cimicifuga; doedecatheon; ferns (most types); filipendula; Gentiana asclepiadea; hemerocallis; hosta; helleborus; Iris kaempferi, I. laevigata, I. pseudacorus, I. sibirica; leucojum; ligularia; Lilium pardalinum; lobelia; lysimachia; lythrum; mimulus; monarda; phlox (border varieties); podophyllum; primula (border primulas); primrose; polyanthus; rheum; rodgersia; Saxifraga umbrosa; schizostylis; sidalcea; trollius.

BULBS

The vast majority of bulbs need well-drained conditions and are not ideally suited to heavy clay, being highly prone to rotting off during winter in wet soil. The best bets are daffodils, galanthus (snowdrops) and leucojum (snowflakes), but even these will appreciate some soil-improvement to reduce waterlogging and speed up drainage, as will all other bulbs. A far wider range of plants will be happy on clay soil if you improve the drainage and add organic material, so that the soil is not exceptionally wet and heavy. There are all degrees of clay soil, from pure solid clay to crumblier and far better drained clayey loams. Not all are as bad as you might think at first sight, but they will all benefit from at least some improvement. The important thing is to open the clay up and improve drainage by working in peat or compost plus sharp sand.

67

Which plants are most suited to dry, chalky soils?

TREES, SHRUBS AND CONIFERS
Acer negundo (box elder); *berberis; buddleia; buxus* (box); *Chamaecyparis lawsoniana* (Lawson's cypress); *cistus* (sun rose); *cotoneaster; deutzia; euonymus; fagus* (beech); *forsythia; hebe; helianthemum; hibiscus; hypericum; junipers; kolkwitzia; laburnum; lavandual* (lavender); *ligustrum* (privet); *malus* (flowering crab apples); *mahonia; olearia; paeonia* (tree paeonies); *philadelphus* (mock-orange); pines; *potentilla;* prunus (flowering cherries, and Portugal laurel); *pyracantha; rhus* (sumach); *ribes* (flowering currant); *rosa* (shrub roses); *rosmarinus* (rosemary); *santolina; senecia; spartium* (Spanish broom); *spiraea; syringa* (lilac); *taxus* (yew); *Thuja plicata* (good hedging conifer); *weigela.*

CLIMBERS AND WALL-COVERING SHRUBS
clematis (especially the strong-growing *Clematis montana*); *Cotoneaster horizontalis; lonicera* (honeysuckles); *Polygonum baldschuanicum; pyracantha.*

BORDER PLANTS
Acanthus; achillea; arabis; agapanthus; alstroemeria; anchusa; bergenia; dianthus (garden pinks); *dictamnus; echinops; eremurus; eryngium; gypsophila; iberis; Iris germanica* (the popular, bearded 'flag' irises) and *I. unguiculais* (also called *I. stylosa*); *linum; nepeta; sedum; sempervivum; thymus* (thymes); *kniphofia* (red-hot poker); *oenothera; Papever orientale* (oriental poppy); *penstemon; pulsatilla; romneva; Stachys lanata; verbascum; veronica.*

BULBS
Most spring bulbs enjoy the extra-free drainage of a chalk soil, most particularly such sun-loving dwarf bulbs as *Anemone blanda, chionodoxa, crocus, Iris reticulata, I. histirioides, I. danfordiae* and the 'species' tulips, all of which enjoy the good summer baking they will get in a dry soil.

Summer-flowering bulbs (such as the lilies) may well need plenty of organic material (such as peat) added to very dry soils, to help them through droughts. If this is done, lime-tolerant lilies, such as *Lilium regale, L. henryi, L. candidum,* and the various trumpet-flowered hybrids, will appreciate the well-drained conditions. But beware: some lilies hate lime; so check before planting.

Most alpine plants also thrive on well-drained chalk soils, so that a rock garden is an excellent choice as a garden feature. The stronger-growing rock plants may also be used in borders and on dry sunny banks. These include *Alyssum saxatile, arabis, armeria, aubrietia, Campanula carpatica, C. postcharskvana, Dianthus deltoides, Geranium cinereum, G. sanguineum, helianthemum* and *Polygonum vaccinifolium.*

2

5

6

3

4

Plants for dry chalky soils:
1. *Sempervivum arachnoideum (houseleek). Good rock plant.*
2. *Pulsatilla vulgaris.*
3. *Chionodoxa luciliae.*
Most dwarf bulbs do well on chalk.
4. *Saxifraga aizoon. Chalk also suits most rock plants.*
5. *Sedum Spathulifolium variety 'Purpureum' (stonecrop).*
6. *Anemone blanda (white form).*

2

3

Plants for dry sandy soils:
1. Mesembryanthemum criniflorum
(Livingstone daisy). Needs as warm and sunny a
site as possible to flower really well.
2. Spartium junceum (Spanish broom). Also a
good shrub for seaside gardens. Flowers over a
long period during summer.
3. Chionodoxa luciliae. Most dwarf bulbs thrive
in sandy soils as the free-draining conditions suit
them perfectly.
4. Genista lydia. A very free flowering dwarf
broom, ideal for large rock gardens, trailing
over retaining walls or ground cover.
5. Senicio greyii. All grey-leaf plants do well on
dry soils.

1

What are the best plants for dry sandy soils?

TREES, SHRUBS AND CONIFERS

Acer negundo (box elder); *ailanthus; berberis; betula* (birch); *calluna* (heathers); *caryopteris; ceanothus; cistus* (sun rose); *cotoneaster; cytisus* (brooms); *elaeagnus; erica* (heathers); *escallonia; genista* (brooms); *gleditsia, hebe, helianthemum; hibiscus; ilex* (hollies); *juniperus* (junipers); *kerria; lavandula; mahonia; olearia; paeonia* (tree paeonies); *philadelphus; pinus* (pines); *potentilla; robinia; romneya; quercus* (oak); *Salix caprea; santolina; Spartium junceum* (Spanish broom); *tamarix; ulex* (gorse).

CLIMBERS

jasminum (jasmines); *lonicera* (honeysuckles); *Polygonum baldschuanicum* (Russian vine); *parthenocissus* (Virginia creeper, Boston ivy); climbing and rambling *roses*.

BORDER PLANTS

Acanthus; achillea; agapanthus; alstronemeria; anchusa; bergenia; dianthus (garden pinks); *echinops; eremurus; euphorbia; eryngium; Iris 'germanica'* (the popular, bearded irises); *kniphofia* (red-hot poker); *linum, lupinus* (lupins); *nepeta; oenothera; Papaver orientale* (oriental poppy); *penstemon; sedum; sempervivum; Stachys lanata; verbascum; veronica.*

BULBS

Almost all bulbs will appreciate the extra-sharp drainage of sandy soil (the Dutch nurserymen grow their bulbs in well-enriched sandy soils). But bear in mind that summer-flowering bulbs may suffer from drought problems if moisture-holding materials are not added to the soil.

ROCK PLANTS

These enjoy well-drained conditions and are therefore good choices. The comments on alpines in the section on plants for dry, chalky soils apply here.

If your sandy soil is acid (as many are) and if you add plenty of organic material (peat, compost, leaf mould etc.) in order to reduce summer drought problems, then a wide range of lovely lime-hating plants and shrubs will grow very happily.

4

5

1

2

Plants for coastal gardens:
1. Herlianthemums (rock roses). Easy rock plants or ground cover.
2. Cytisus kewensis. Superb dwarf broom, suitable for a large rock garden and good ground cover.
3. Crocosmia masonorum.
4. Spartium junceum (Spanish broom). Flowers June -August.
5. Fuchsia riccartonii. Other hardy fuchsias are equally good.

Which plants are most likely to do well in exposed coastal gardens?

Most of the plants listed here will prove equally good choices for exposed, windy, inland gardens. But bear in mind that inland areas are generally colder in winter than coastal areas. The further inland, the more care you should take to select the hardiest plants, avoiding any which are slightly tender.

Try to avoid tall, floppy border plants which may need staking in windy situations. Where winds are especially strong, make particular use of low-spreading plants and shrubs, such as the stronger-growing rock plants, heathers and other ground-cover plants. Remember, however, always to include some taller wind-tolerant plants and shrubs among the low spreaders for variety and contrast.

Take equal care over flowering bulb selections, as many of the taller types are apt to be blown flat on very windy sites, especially the tallest and largest-flowered tulips and daffodils and tall summer bulbs like lilies and gladioli. Dwarf bulbs, on the other hand, are excellent choices. Bulbs in general tolerate salty seaside

3

conditions well, since they disappear below ground for much of the year and salt cannot build up on their annually-replaced leaves.

TREES, SHRUBS AND CONIFERS

buddleia; calluna (heather); *cistus* (sun rose); *cotoneaster; crataegus* (ornamental thorn); *Cupressocyparis leylandii* (Leyland cypress, good hedging choice); *cytisus* (broom); *elaeagnus; erica* (heather); *escallonia* (good evergreen flowering hedge); *Euonymus fortunei, E. japonicus; fuschia; garrva; genista* (broom); *hebe; helianthemum; hydrangea; hypericum; ilex* (holly); *juniperus* (juniper); *lavandula* (lavender); *olearia* (daisy bush); *pinus* (pine); *potentilla; pyracantha; rosa* (shrub roses); *rosmarinus* (rosemary); *santolina; senecio; sorbus* (mountain ash); *spartium* (Spanish broom); *spriaea; tamarix; ulex* (gorse); *viburnum; yucca.*

CLIMBERS AND WALL-COVERING SHRUBS

Polygonum baldschuanicum; pyracantha; climbing *roses.*

BORDER PLANTS

achillea; agapanthus; armeria; alstroemeria; alyssum; arabis; artemisia; aster (dwarf Michaelmas daisies); *anemone; aubrietia; bergenia; campanula* (spreading rock-plant types); *centaurea; crocosmia* (montbretia); *dianthus* (garden pink); *echinops; eryngium; euphorbia; geranium* (border types, and rock plants); *gypsophila; Iris 'germanica'* (bearded border iris varieties); *kniphofia* (red-hot poker); *lathyrus* (sweet pea); *lavatera; limonium; linaria; linum; lobelia; mesembryantheumum; oenothera; penstemon; physostegia; pulsatilla; sedum; sempervivum; stachys; veronica.*

4

5

1

2

3

4

5

6

Plants for coastal gardens:
1. Armeria maritima (thrift). Suitable for a large rock garden, and a good border-edging plant.
2. Hydrangea macrophylla variety 'Preziosa'. All hydrangeas stand up to salt spray well and thrive best of all in the milder coastal areas of the south and west.

Plants for small gardens:
3. Malus 'Golden Hornet'. Small flowering crab-apple with highly decorative yellow fruits.
4. Abies balsamea 'Hudsonia'. One of the neatest of the dwarf conifers. Choose carefully for small gardens as some 'dwarf' conifers can grow quite large.
5. Acer palmatum 'Atropurpureum'. A truly elegant slow-growing small tree or large shrub. Seldom gets too large even for the smallest of gardens.
6. Daphne mezereum. A popular winter-flowering shrub with sweetly scented flowers.

75

What are the best plants for a small garden?

Rock plants and dwarf bulbs are ideal, providing plenty of colour from a small planting space. Dwarf conifers are also good and go well with heathers; choose dwarf conifers with extra care (especially for small rock gardens), as some grow much faster than other varieties.

Be wary of the larger border plants, whose wide-spreading foliage may take up more space in a small garden than their flowers warrant. But most importantly, take care with trees and shrubs, which are much more likely to cause long-term space problems than border plants. Always check on ultimate spread as well as eventual height.

SMALL TREES

Acer palmatum varieties, *A. griseum;* flowering *cherries* (notably, the narrow column-shaped *Prunus 'Amanogawa'* for very tight spaces); *Cotoneaster 'Cornubia'* (evergreen, red berries); *Crataegus 'Paul's Scarlet'* (red may-blossom); *Juniperus virginiana 'Skyrocket'* (a very slim-growing juniper); *Laburnum vossii; malus* (flowering crabs); *Pyrus salicifolia 'Pendula'* (weeping silver-leaved pear); *Salix caprea 'Pendula'* (small weeping willow); *Sorbus aucuparia* varieties (mountain ash).

SMALL CONIFERS

Chamaecyparis pisifera 'Boulevard'; Picea glauca albetiana 'Conica'; Thuja occidentalis 'Rheingold'; Thuja plicata 'Stoneham Gold'.

SMALL AND SLOW-GROWING SHRUBS

Abelia; acer (slow-growing Japanese maples); *azalea* (evergreen); *Berberis darwinii; buxus* (box, a good dwarf hedge); *calluna* (heater); *camellia; choisya; cistus* (sun rose); *cytisus* (dwarf brooms); *hebe; helianthemum; hydrangea; Hypericum 'Hidcote' lavandula* (lavender); *Magnolia stellate; mahonia; Philadelphus 'Manteau d'Hermine'* (dwarf mock-orange); *potentilla; rhododendron* (dwarf varieties); *ribes* (flowering currant); rose (miniature varieties); *skimmia; spiraea; Thuja Viburnum tinus.*

1. Potentilla 'Red ace'. Flowers non-stop all summer long.
2. Sweet scented Daphne retusa.
3. Hypericum olympicum.
4. Camellia williamsii 'Donation'

4

CLIMBERS

Be wary, in very small gardens, of planting the very fastest growing climber, such as *Polygonum baldschuanicum, Hydrangea petiolaris, parthenoccisus, Clematis montana* and *Vitis coignetiae*. Otherwise, most ornamental climbers are highly suitable for adding extra colour and interest on the walls and fences of small gardens.

Which plants must have acid

(non-limy) soil?

The following are the most commonly grown lime-haters. If the garden is limy, they may be grown in tubs or raised beds filled with a non-limy 'ericaceous' potting compost (available from garden centres).

TREES AND SHRUBS

Azalea; calluna (summer-flowering heathers); *camellia; daboecia* (heather); *enkianthus; erica* (heather; the summer-flowering types need acid soil, but the winter-flowering ones do not mind lime); *eucryphia; fothergilla; gualtheria; kalmia; nyssa; pernettya; philesia; pieris; rhododenron; vaccinium.*

BORDER PLANTS AND BULBS

gentiana (the autumn-flowering Himalayan gentians, such as *Gentiana sino-ornata*, must have acid soil; but the spring and summer gentians enjoy limy soils); *dwarf Iris 'Pacific Coast'* or *'California'* hybrids; *Lilium auratum, L. speciosum*, and the *'Oriental' lily* hybrids (plus some other less common species; so always check on soil needs); *lithospermum; Meconopsis betoniciflia, M. grandis* (and other blue Himalayan poppies).

Do not feed these lime-hating plants with bonemeal, which contains lime (John Innes Base is a good, balanced, lime-free fertilizer). And do not use spent mushroom compost, which is limy, as a soil-improving material where lime-haters are to be planted.

Azaleas provide a brilliant splash of colour in late spring, rivalled only by the large flowered rhododendron hybrids for sheer exotic opulence. But remember that they need acid soil.

PLANTS IN CONTAINERS

Do plants in containers require special care and attention?

A container is not a natural habitat for any plant. Many of the troubles that afflict plants in the garden border (such as poor drainage, drought and shortage of nutrients, are more likely to strike down plants in pots, tubs, troughs, window boxes and hanging baskets. Extra care when planting and special attention to their later needs is therefore essetial.

3

2

4

5

1. Tulipa kaufmanniana 'Fritz Kreisler'. Dwarf tulips are ideal choices for tubs and windowboxes.
2. Juniperus communis 'Compressa'. An extremely slow growing dwarf conifer (less than an inch a year). Excellent for planting in a tub or trough garden with rock plants.
3. Saxifraga apiculata. Dainty alpines make marvellous miniature gardens planted up in containers.
4. Rhododendron 'Blue Tit'. Dwarf rhododendrons are good in tubs.
5. Begonia semperflorens. A popular bedding plant for tubs, windowboxes and hanging baskets. Does well in shady situations.

81

DRAINAGE

Drainage is the most vital point. Make sure that your plant containers have plenty of drainage holes, large enough so that they will not readily become blocked; otherwise roots may rot in waterlogged compost. Place broken crocks, small stones or chippings in a layer over these holes, to prevent the growing compost from clogging them.

Always stand tubs and troughs on bricks, stones or other low supports, to keep the base of the container off the ground and further ensure that excess water may drain freely. Similarly, a window box which is going to sit on a ledge should have strips of wood (or other low supports) underneath, in order to keep the drainage holes off the ledge.

SOIL

Never use garden soil in containers. It may be of a poor quality, heavy and slow-draining, and short of moisture-holding organic material; and therefore highly prone to waterlogging in wet weather and to drying out fast during hot spells. Your garden soil will almost certainly contain weed seeds, and possibly weed roots, which will cause problems later. And plant pests and disease spores, which may also be present in garden soil, can wreak havoc in a container. Instead, use a peat-based or soil-based potting compost, which should be comparatively sterile, free-draining and enriched with a balanced dose of plant foods. Peat-based compost is most suitable for fast-growing plants for temporary seasonal displays, such as bedding plants and bulbs. Permanent plants, such as shrubs and conifers, will generally do better with a soil-based compost, which will remain in good condition and retain a store of plant foods longer than peat. And do remember to use a lime-free 'ericaceous' potting compost when growing lime-hating plants, such as rhododendrons, azaleas, and camellias, in tubs.

WATERING

Plants in containers need much more frequent watering in dry weather than plants in the open ground. During hot weather or prolonged drought, check them at least once a day. Hanging baskets, in particular, quickly become parched and may need watering twice a day in a hot spell; if they are allowed to become bone-dry they will be difficult to re-moisten. Watering with a can is not the most effective method. It is better to lift down the basket and

1

2

3

4

5

6

7

1. Tulipa greigili 'Red Riding Hood'. Excellent short-stemmed choice for tubs and windowboxes. The purple-striped leaves are an added attraction.

Other good dwarf tulips for planting in containers include Tulipa praestans 'Fusilier', T. kaufmanniana varieties (waterlily tulips) and other T. greigii hybrids such as 'Cape Cod' (red and yellow flowers) and 'Plaisir' (cream and red)

2. Tulipa kaufmanniana variety 'Stresa'. These dwarf 'waterlily' tulips are particularly useful for early colour, flowering from March onwards. Other good varieties include 'Heart's Delight' (red and white) and 'Shakespeare' (apricot and salmon-orange).

3. Impatiens (busy Lizzie). Good annual bedding plant for tubs, windowboxes and hanging baskets in shady situations.

4. and *6.* Heathers are good in tubs and troughs, planted with dwarf or slow growing conifers. And if your garden soil is limy, a tub of lime-free 'ericaceous' potting compost will allow you to grow some of the colourful lime-hating, summer flowering heathers around the feet of a small conifer.

5. Trailing impatiens (busy Lizzies) look good in tubs and hanging baskets.

7. Lobelias are ideal for hanging baskets and windowboxes.

83

dunk it in a bowl of water until the compost is well soaked. Never hang a newly-planted basket in a sunny position straight away. Give it a soaking, and keep it in a shady place for at least a couple of days, to let the plants settle in. With moss-lined wire baskets, a saucer placed on the moss in the bottom of the basket, before filling with compost, will act as a reservoir, thus keeping the compost moist for a little longer between waterings.

FEEDING

Regular watering quickly washes plant nutrients out of the compost in containers; so containers also require more frequent doses of fertilizer than garden borders. Bear in mind, also, that a peat compost will loose its goodness much faster than a soil-based one. Give bedding displays in containers regular feeds throughout the growing season with a liquid fertilizer (a high-potash feed, such as liquid tomato fertilizer, will promote free flowering). Liquid fertilizer may be used to give shrubs in tubs the occasional quick boost, but these permanent plants will also appreciate a couple of top-dressings a year (in spring and autumn) of a longer-lasting, solid, balanced fertilizer.

What are the best plants

for containers?

Bedding plants and spring bulbs are widely used in window boxes, tubs, and troughs for spring and summer colour. Try to choose a selection to give some variety of plant height and growth habit within the display – ideally, taller plants (or bulbs) to stand above the bushier sorts, plus trailing plants to spill over the edges of the container.

In window boxes, avoid the tallest plants and bulbs, which will block light from the window and may be damaged by wind and rain on exposed ledges. Choose the dwarf 'rockery' varieties of narcissus and tulip for spring, together with other sturdy, short-stemmed bulbs, such as hyacinths and crocus.
For hanging baskets, trailers are particularly useful (with some bushier plants for variety). Good choices include trailing lobelias, ivy-leaved pelargoniums, drooping-stemmed fuchsia varieties such as *Fuchsia 'Cascade'*, trailing 'Pendula' begonias, and any trailing varieties of petunia.

Evergreens are the best permanent plants for tubs and troughs, providing an interesting feature all year round. Choose spectacular flowering evergreen foliage. Rhododendrons are an ideal choice, and so are the glossy-leaved and exotic camellias (especially if your garden soil is limy and unsuited to these gorgeous lime-haters). Dwarf conifers with colourful foliage for winter interest are also good, as are rock plants; and they go perfectly together to make a miniature rock garden in a large tub or trough.

Planting-up a hanging basket: Line wire baskets with moss (not necessary for solid plastic containers) and fill with a peat based potting compost.

Place plants in the sides of the basket as you build up the moss and compost inside. Use trailing plants around the sides.

Finish off with bushy plants in the top. Water and place in shade for a day or two before/hanging.

2

The following chapter deals with major garden features such as lawns, hedges, ponds, rock gardens and raised beds. It is vital to get these main structural components of the garden right otherwise they can cause endless problems later on.

1. Berberis stenophylla hedge. This plant makes a beautiful informal flowering hedge, a cascade of golden-yellow flower in spring if not clipped too neatly. But in a small garden a fast growing and bushy hedging plant like this could well cause trouble as it grows up.

2. Clipped green and golden yew hedges. Yew is slow growing but makes a superlative hedge well worth waiting for.

1

85

MAJOR GARDEN FEATURES

Most important of all is thorough soil-penetration. Few things in gardening are more disappointing than a struggling, slow-growing hedge which fails, year after year, to provide the shelter and privacy you want.

Ideally, dig a trench where the hedge is to go, to at least one spade-depth. Break up the bottom of the trench with a garden fork and work in humus material (compost, leaf mould, well-rotten manure, peat, etc.) Refill the trench with soil, mixing in plenty of humus material as you go. Do this well in advance of planting, if possible, to allow the soil plenty of time to settle. When you come to plant, sprinkle a small handful of balanced compound fertilizer around the sides and bottom of each planting hole and some moist peat or garden compost over and around the roots of each plant. This is a recipe for perfection, and well worth sticking to where something as important as a hedge is concerned. Failing this, at least be sure to work plenty of humus material into the soil as you plant, and sprinkle some around the roots. In particular, work some peat or compost well into the base of each planting hole. And do not forget the fertilizer.

Planting distances vary from one type of hedging plant to another and are too numerous to list here. Catalogues usually give them, gardening reference books do, and nurserymen ought to be able to advise. About 18in apart is the average, 1ft for the slowest-growing and smallest hedge types, and up to 2ft for the fastest-growing. The popular and very strong-growing Leyland cypress (*Cupressocyparis leylandii*) may go in up to 4ft apart if a quick tall screen is desired, but it will take longer to make a dense hedge than if planted at 2ft.

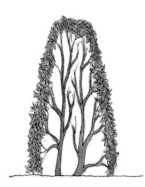

Above: For the best results (fast and healthy growth) when planting a hedge, dig a trench to a spade-depth, break up the soil in the base of the trench with a fork, and refill with soil enriched with humus and fertiliser.
Left: Clip hedges narrower at the top than the bottom, to help discourage a bare base and top-heavy growth developing.

Small plants of hedging material generally settle in faster and grow quicker than large ones; so buy them 1-2ft tall, save money, and get a better hedge in the long run. Prune back deciduous hedging plants and stronger-growing, straggly evergreens (except for conifers) by about one-third, after planting, to encourage bushy growth low down. Keep new hedges well watered during dry weather, and feed with a balanced compound fertilizer in spring and autumn to boost growth.

Trim the tops and sides of hedging plants from an early age to ensure neat, dense growth. In particular, do not let *C.leylandii* conifer get too bushy before you start trimming, as it can make phenomenal side growth once it gets going and hates being cut back into bare wood late in life. Do not forget to stop upward growth when it reaches the desired height; otherwise the hedge may get out of hand. With the *Leyland* conifer, if you want a neat formal hedge, allow it to grow 12-18in above the desired height and then cut it down by 12-18in. This will encourage a solid, bushy top, instead of a thin straggly one.

Once established, formal hedges should be trimmed at least twice a year (generally in mid-summer and early autumn) to keep them neat; strong growers, like privet, need more frequent trimming. Flowering hedges should be trimmed after their flowering is over. With berrying hedges (e.g. cotoneaster and pyracantha) prune back the longest shoots after flowering, leaving shorter flowering shoots to produce berries.

Aim to trim hedges so that they are thick at the base, becoming gradually thinner towards the top. This discourages them from growing top-heavy and bare at the bottom (a common fault with neglected hedges).

What should go into the making and maintenance of a good lawn?

As with hedges (and all planting and sowing operations), so with lawns, it is soil-preparation which counts most in the long term.

First, dig out or kill off the roots of any perennial weeds such as dandelion, dock, couch grass, nettle, and bindweed. If using weedkiller, choose one which will not linger in the soil.

Turves should be laid staggered, like brickwork. Gently firm turf down using a plank as shown.

Rake finely crumbled moist peat into any gaps/between turves to encourage fast bonding.

Second, dig, fork and rake the soil into a fine, crumbly condition, adding some humus material (e.g. peat or compost) if it is a 'problem' soil (heavy clay, dry sand or shallow, chalky soil). On heavy clays, working in plenty of coarse sand, in addition to humus materials, will improve soil drainage and reduce worries over wet, muddy turf later. Finally, top-dress with a pre-seeding lawn fertilizer or a balanced compound fertilizer and rake in.

Now you are ready to sow, or lay turves (which is much more expensive, but does provide a more instant lawn). For shady areas, choose one of the special shade-tolerant grass-seed mixes now widely available from seed catalogues and garden shops. The best time to sow grass seed or lay turf is during the cool days of spring and early autumn, but you can do it in

87

summer, provided you remember to water during dry spells.

Keep lawns in good condition with regular feeds to replace the goodness taken out of the soil by grass roots and carried off to the compost heap in the form of grass clippings. Specialized lawn fertilizers are available, but a general balanced compound fertilizer will do.

If poor soil drainage and muddy grass are a problem with an existing lawn,

spiking the turf with a garden fork in autumn will aid winter drainage. Spreading and brushing-in peat and coarse sand, after spiking, will make matters better still. On dry soils, where parched grass is a worry in summer, spike the lawn and brush in moist peat, but not sand.

Persistent lawn weeds (such as dandelions and docks) should be either dug out with a hand-fork or painted with a 'spot' weedkiller.

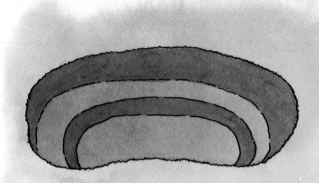

Creating a garden pond: Excavate to at least 2ft. to give enough depth of water to prevent the pond freezing solid in cold weather. Create shallower shelves around the sides for 'marginal' aquatic plants which will not grow in deep water.

Remove sharp stones and spread a layer of sand or newspapers over the base and sides of your excavation to cushion the lining sheet. Allow for a generous overlap of 2-3ft. all round the sides when buying the sheet.

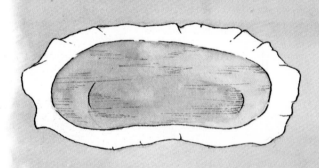

Once filled with water, leave for a few days and check for dropping water levels indicating leaks. When you are sure the liner is not leaking, trim the edges of the pond liner, weighting it down and disguising it with stones, slabs or a layer of soil.

Sink aquatic plants in soil-filled baskets into the pond. Do not drop them straight into the depths. First stand the baskets on bricks in the water and gradually move them deeper. Do not introduce fish for at least six to eight weeks.

How should you go about creating a garden pond?

The cheapest and easiest method is to line your pool with strong plastic or synthetic rubber sheeting. Special heavy-duty lining sheets are available from garden centres and aquatic centres. Do not try to cut costs with ordinary thin polythene sheet. The better quality the sheet, the longer it is likely to last without leaking.

Buy enough sheeting to line the pond and overlap the edges by 1ft or more. Trim a little if necessary, and bury the overlap under the soil, rocks, or flagstones. Before lining, smooth the sides and base of the excavation and remove any sharp stones; then spread a layer of sand, or thick layers of

newspaper, over the bottom and sides to cushion the lining sheet against the possibility of puncturing.

The pond should be 2ft deep to prevent it from freezing solid in winter, with shelving up to 6-8in in one corner for marginal aquatic plants which do not like deep water. Aquatics, such as water lilies, should be sunk in soil-filled baskets. Allow at least six weeks after filling with water before introducing fish.

Never allow autumn leaves to collect in the pond; keep skimming them off. And if the surface freezes over in winter, make a small hole and keep this open to prevent fish and plants suffocating from lack of oxygen. Never break ice if the pond contains fish; instead, melt a hole with hot water.

What is the correct way to lay paths and patios?

Paving slabs are simpler to lay than concrete or other materials (except gravel). And a good foundation is absolutely essential. The deeper and better compacted the foundation, the steadier the flagstones will be and the fewer problems you are likely to encounter later.

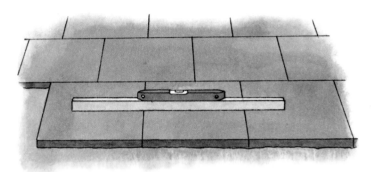

Use a straight-edged board and a spirit level to ensure that paving slabs are laid level. Lay on a bed of sand for stability.

Unless the paving is to be raised up above soil level, excavate the ground to a depth of 2-4in, depending on how deep you plan to make the foundations. Spread, level and tamp down a layer of hardcore; then bed the slabs on to a final layer of sand or (for greater stability and permanence) blobs of concrete mix, spreading a spot of concrete for each corner of the slab and a fifth spot in the centre.

As you lay the slabs, check constantly with a straight-edged plank (or, better still, with a spirit level) to ensure that they are level. Paths and patios alongside house walls should always slope gently away from the house, so that rain water runs away from the wall.

For gravel areas, excavate and spread hardcore 2-4in deep. Make sure that the hardcore is well tamped down, and then spread the gravel on top. A brick or concrete edging may be required to prevent the gravel from spreading on to adjoining lawns or borders.

How do you build raised beds?

Raised beds may be built with all kinds of materials: brick, stone, blocks, old railway sleepers, etc. Dry-stone raised beds look particularly attractive, with plants growing through the gaps along the sides.

Raised beds need not be very high to help break up the flatness of a level garden site. And even a height of just 8-12in will help to ensure well-drained soil conditions within the bed, to suit rock plants, dwarf conifers and the fussier rock-garden bulbs. But it is more usual to build to seat-height (about 17-18in) so that the walls may be used as handy sitting places when weeding, tending the plants or simply admiring the display. The most important point, unless you are building only a very low bed, is to lay solid foundations. They will greatly increase stability and reduce the risk of subsidence. Dig out a trench where the walls are to go, a little wider than the thickness of the wall and 5-6in deep. Fill with concrete mix and mortar the bottom course of the wall on to this. Remember that dry-stone walls, built without mortar, should always lean back at an angle against the soil behind (so that the bed is narrower at the top than at the bottom).

And when building mortared walls, leave some half-brick size planting holes so that you can plant the sides of the bed as well as the top, for maximum colour and interest.

Always thoroughly fork over the ground in the base of the raised bed before filling it with soil or compost to ensure free drainage. On heavy, slow-draining clay soils, work some hardcore, rubble, chipping or coarse sand into the ground for improved drainage.

Finally, fill the raised bed with either garden soil enriched with peat or compost, plus a compound balanced fertilizer, or with bags of ready-mixed potting compost. If you plan to grow lime-haters such as rhododendrons, and if your garden soil is limy, use lime-free 'ericaceous' potting compost.

Note: The advice on building walls for raised beds (especially the need for good foundations and the need to slope dry-laid walls backwards) applies equally to retaining walls built to create terraces or hold back steep banks.

Excavate and prepare solid foundations and cement the first course to the foundations.

Fill in with either bought-in potting compost or with garden soil enriched with peat or compost and compound fertiliser.

Ensure good drainage by breaking up the soil in the base and digging in grit or chippings.

89

What precautions can you take to ensure that wooden fences stay in good condition and last as long as possible?

It is vital to protect the base of a wooden fence, as this is where it is most prone to rot. Always thoroughly soak the bottoms of fencing posts in wood-preservative. Then, either set them into concrete-filled holes or into metal, spiked post-holders which have been driven into the ground. And do not forget to protect the tops of posts against rain with wooden caps, to stop water from soaking into the grain and inducing rot.

Make sure that the bottoms of wooden fencing panels do not touch the ground, or they, too, will rot, And take care not to pile soil up against either posts or panels when cultivating and planting garden borders.

Do not forget to paint the fence with wood preserver every two or three years to prolong its life. Creosote will damage plants if splashed on their leaves; so where plants are growing on the fence or close by, use a non-harmful water-based preservative (garden shops will advise on all available brands).

What are the basic rules for building rock gardens?

Always choose a sunny site for your rock garden, as few alpines will tolerate shade well. It should not be up against a house wall, where rainwater from eaves or leaky gutters will drip on to the plants — another thing that rock plants will not stand. Similarly, avoid sites overhung by trees whose branches will drip rainwater and drop soggy autumn leaves on to the alpines.

Rock plants hate to sit in wet soil during winter and will quickly rot in such conditions. On the other hand, they do not particularly enjoy being dry at the roots in spring and summer. If the garden soil is not naturally fast-draining (especially if it is at all clayey) work in lashings of coarse sand and grit, as much as a bucketful to every bucket of soil if the soil is particularly heavy. At the same time, to every bucketful of this fast-draining mixture add a quarter of a bucket of peat, to hold summer moisture in and prevent roots from drying out in hot weather. If your soil is naturally sandy or stony and fast-draining, you need add only the peat. On acid soils, mix in some ground chalk or limestone chips, as most alpines prefer a slightly limy soil (except for dwarf rhododendrons, summer-flowering heathers and a few other lime-haters).

On a level site, the soil should be mounded up above the surrounding ground, to ensure good winter drainage. Soil excavated for the foundations of paths and patios will come in handy here. Rock plants will, of course, be equally happy in a raised alpine bed as an excellent alternative to the traditional rock garden. On steep slopes, which are always fast-draining, raising the soil level should not be necessary; simply improve the soil as recommended above.

After planting, spread a layer of stone chippings between the plants and tuck some chippings under their foliage. This will help to keep the soil moist and cool in summer, while preventing the low-growing plants and their flowers from becoming mud-splashed in rainy weather. Rocks are not essential for the health of the plants, but they do add greatly to the character of the alpine garden. There is no space here for a detailed discussion on the art of arranging rock and creating natural-looking rock gardens. But bear in mind that the aim is to produce something which looks like a natural rock-outcrop, not a rounded mound dotted with odd little stones, lumps of concrete and half-bricks.

Choose plants for smaller rock gardens carefully, as many of the more common rock plants are very strong growers and fast spreaders. Equally, choose dwarf conifers warily, as some so-called dwarf varieties can grow quite large over the years. One of the neatest and loveliest of them, suitable for the very smallest of rock gardens, is the very slow-growing spire-shaped *Juniperus communis 'Compressa'*.

2

1. Use plants to disguise the hard edges of a patio and blend it into the garden. The two conifers are aged specimens of the very slow-growing Juniperus communis 'Compressa'.
2. Thuja orientalis 'Aurea Nana'. Dwarf conifers look at home on rock gardens and raised beds. But for a small rock garden choose carefully as some grow much larger than others.
Left: Sectional view through a typical rock garden, showing the basic construction method.
3. Saxifraga aizoon 'Rosea', a dainty little alpine plant.

How do you ensure good crops from the vegetable garden?

SOIL

Most important of all is to make sure that your vegetable-growing area is in a sunny site and that the soil is in good condition, or in 'good heart' as seasoned gardeners say. The ideal to strive for is a deep top-soil which is free-draining (not prone to waterlogging after heavy rain) and well enriched with compost, manure and other humus-adding materials. It should dig easily, crumble readily into a fine breadcrumb 'tilth', and contain enough organic matter to hold summer moisture and sustain beneficial soil organisms.

If you have one of the problem soils discussed in this book, do your utmost to improve it as recommended; otherwise successful vegetable growing will always prove a struggle in one way or another.

Vegetables take a lot out of the ground, and even a good, loamy soil will need regular infusions of compost or manure. If you let the soil run short of organic matter, it will become increasingly lifeless and infertile, demanding ever-greater doses of fertilizers to produce adequate crops. Remember that garden compost is not only good for the soil, but virtually free; the more of it you make and get into the ground, the less you will need to spend on expensive fertilizers.

SOWING

Do not be in too much of a hurry to sow and plant. Gardening books, seed catalogues and seed packet instructions tend to be optimistic, recommending sowing and planting dates early in the season, which may not suit your soil or the situation of your garden, or the weather conditions of a particular year. Always wait until the soil has started to dry out, warmed up and become more easily worked after the winter rains. If the spring weather is unusually cold and wet, you should be particularly 'laid back', delaying sowing until the conditions are right. Seeds sown into cold, wet ground will produce poor results or may fail altogether; later sowings will often catch up with, and surpass, early sowings made under adverse conditions.

Remember that autumn or winter rough-digging and ridging-up on clay soils will render them crumblier and more suitable for sowing (thanks to the action of frosts) when spring comes around.

You will also be able to sow and plant earlier, in warmer and drier soil, if you cover the vegetable beds with weighted-down polythene sheets in mid-winter (to ward off heavy rains and trap the warming rays of the sun). For still earlier sowings and crops, use polythene cloches to warm up the soil and protect early seedlings.

CROP ROTATION

Crop rotation is vital for a healthy and productive vegetable garden. Moving crops to different parts of the plot each year helps to prevent the build-up of pests and diseases that occur when a particular crop is grown in the same patch of soil year after year and therefore reduces the need for expensive insecticides and fungicides.

Crop rotation also cuts the cost of fertilizers as a crop which needs a particular plant food may follow another crop which does not use up that nutrient in the soil. The best example is that of peas and beans. These do not need much nitrogen, since their roots manufacture this nutrient, with the help of certain micro-organisms. After cropping, cut peas and beans off at soil-level, leaving their nitrogen-rich roots in the ground. The following spring, plant nitrogen-hungry brassicas (cabbage, sprouts, cauliflowers, etc.) where the beans and peas were, and these will make use both of the nitrogen that the beans and peas did not need and of the extra nitrogen produced by the roots of the pea and bean crops.

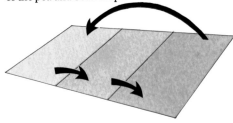

Typical crop rotation plan: Root crops follow brassicas. The brassicas follow peas, beans and other miscellaneous crops, and these follow the root crops.

What are the popular needs of different vegetable crops?

Most vegetable crops will do reasonably well if sown or planted into sunny, well-cultivated and humus-enriched soil, watered during dry spells, kept relatively weed-free, and fed with a balanced compound fertilizer. Learning the individual preferences of different vegetables is, however, important if you want to get the best from your kitchen garden. A specialist handbook on vegetable growing is a very worthwhile investment, which will pay for itself many times over in improved crops. But, as a rough guide, the following general notes should be of some help in avoiding basic mistakes.

POTATOES

Potatoes make an excellent first crop for newly-cleared ground, as the dense foliage smothers weeds, and they yield a reasonable crop even on 'problem' soils, provided you work in plenty of compost or well-rotted manure. The tubers are less prone to the common disease, potato scab, in acid soils; so never lime the ground before planting. On limy soils, dig in lashings of compost or manure to conteract the liminess.

OTHER ROOT VEGETABLES (CARROT, PARSNIP, ETC.)

Prefer a deep, well-dug and slightly sandy soil. If your top-soil is shallow, stony, or clayey, choose the short-rooted varieties, which will perform better than the long-root varieties in such conditions. Do not add manure to the ground, as it can cause 'fanging' (roots dividing and growing into odd, unusable shapes); add compost or peat instead, if the soil is short of humus material.

ONIONS

Raising onions from seed is slow and often gives poor results if conditions are not just right. Onion sets produce much more reliable results a lot faster. Ideally, you should prepare the soil in autumn, adding compost or manure, to allow it to settle before planting sets in early spring. Feed with a general fertilizer. Do not over-feed in an attempt to get giant bulbs, as smaller ones store better.

BRASSICAS (CABBAGE, CAULIFLOWER, SPROUT, CALABRESE, ETC.)

Most important, all of these must be planted out into firm ground, not loose recently-worked soil; and they need plenty of humus in the ground. Ideally, dig and add compost or manure in autumn and leave the soil to settle during winter and spring, so that it is firm when you come to plant out the seedlings. If the soil is acid, be sure to lime it in late winter, as brassicas hate acid conditions. If digging and manuring has to be done in spring, tread the soil lightly before planting. When planting, always tread soil firmly over the roots. Brassicas need plenty of nitrogen; so give slow-growing plants a boost with dried blood or other nitrogen feeds.

On small vegetable plots and in garden borders grow runner beans on cane 'wigwams'.

PEAS AND BEANS

Prefer well-worked soil with plenty of organic matter (compost, well-rotted manure, spent mushroom compost, etc.) dug in deep, to keep the roots moist during dry summer weather. All crop better and are less prone to disease if well-supplied with potassium; add a little sulphate of potash in addition to a general fertilizer when preparing the ground. Do not feed with nitrogen fertilizers, which these plants do not need and which may encourage excessive leafy growth at the expense of flowering pod-set, and final yield.

In a small garden tomatoes, lettuce, spring onions and some other crops may be grown on paths and patios using grow-bags.

FRUITING VEGETABLES (TOMATO, CUCUMBER, COURGETTE, ETC.)

Well-dug ground with plenty of compost or well-rotted manure is best for these vegetables. They appreciate a little extra potash (for better fruit-production) even more than peas and beans. Give all of them a boost with either a high-potash tomato fertilizer, or a little sulphate of potash.

SALAD CROPS (LETTUCE, SPRING ONIONS, RADISH, CELERY)

These need well-prepared and thoroughly humus-enriched soils, plus regular watering in dry weather, to promote fast succulent growth. Boost slow-growing lettuce and celery with a little dried blood or other nitrogen feed.

How can you ensure good fruit crops?

Remember that fruit trees, bushes and canes will stay in the same patch of ground for many years; so soil preparation and improvement should be as thorough as possible, more so than for seasonal vegetable crops. Always choose the sunniest possible site, to encourage free flowering and fruiting. Dig deep, and work in lots of humus material.

Feeding annually with a general balanced fertilizer in early spring, together with regularly mulching over the root area with compost or well-rotted manure, will help to maintain healthy growth and cropping. If cropping or fruit-quality is poor, give a boost with sulphate of potash fertilizer.

Remember that many apple varieties and most pears will not crop well (and may not crop at all) if planted on their own. Most need to be grown close to another (different) variety which flowers around the same time, so that the two can pollinate one another. Even those varieties which catalogues state will crop on their own generally crop more heavily if another variety is planted nearby. Fruit catalogues and nurserymen will usually advise on suitable choices for good cross-pollination.

APPLES

The most popular choice of fruit tree, apple is one of the easiest to maintain. Choose varieties suitable for your area from catalogues and reference books. Some do better in the south

Comparative heights of apple trees grown on different root-stocks: (a) M27, 4-5ft. (b) M9, 8-9ft. (c) MM106, 10-12ft.

than in the colder north, notably the popular 'Cox's Orange Pippin', which seldom crops well in the north. Do not forget to choose varieties for good cross-pollination.

For neat bushes just 4-5ft tall (ideal for small gardens), buy apples on the ultra-dwarfing rootstock M27. These dwarf bushes crop earlier and yield larger fruits than bigger trees and bushes. If it is necessary to cut back main branches and shoots to improve shape, or to thin out overcrowded branches and encourage strong new growth the following season, this should be done during frost-free weather while the tree is leafless in winter. Dwarf bushes on M27 rootstocks need little pruning, and are therefore a good choice if you do not want to have to worry much about this.

PEARS

Pear trees need warmer sites than apple trees. In cold or windy gardens, especially in the north, pears crop best on sunny walls (fan-trained or as single-stemmed cordons) or in very well-sheltered, sunny corners. Almost all varieties need a different variety nearby to cross-pollinate and ensure good crops. If there is room for only one tree, choose the self-fertile variety, 'Conference' (though even this produces better-quality fruit if cross-pollinated).

General pruning advice for pear trees is the same as for apples, but if they are grown as cordons or fan-trained, then more specialized treatment is required (check with gardening reference books or seek advice when buying).

STONE FRUITS

Damsons are the easiest, cropping well in most gardens. Plums are not such a good bet for colder northern gardens, where they are best given a well-sheltered site or the protection of a wall. The plum-like, richly flavoured gages must have a warm site and are best against a sunny wall, even in the south. These can all be bought on the dwarfing rootstock, 'Pixy'. If not grafted on to dwarfing rootstocks, plums and damsons can grow into quite large sprawling trees. Peaches, nectarines and apricots

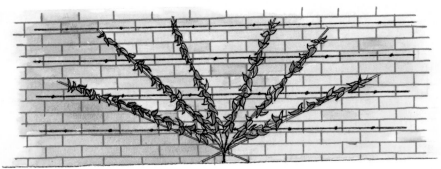

Fan-trained fruit trees may be grown on sunny walls for a space-saving crop (especially useful in a small garden). Peaches, figs, cherries and pears are popular choices.

generally need to be grown on sunny walls, even in warmer regions. In the north they usually need the protection of a lean-to greenhouse or conservatory. It is essential to do any necessary pruning of stone fruits in spring or summer, not in winter, as winter pruning can make these trees susceptible to disease.

BLACK CURRANTS
These are very hardy and happy in most gardens and on most soil types. They enjoy plenty of humus in the soil and an annual spring feed with dried blood or other nitrogen fertilizers. Do not expect a crop on the young shoots in the first year: currants bear fruit on shoots grown during the previous season. Pruning is simple. When planting, cut all stems to 3in. Once cropping starts, cut about a third of the shoots, each autumn removing older branches which have fruited and leaving young, light-brown shoots to crop the following year.

GOOSEBERRIES
These are easily grown in all parts of the country and will even crop in partial shade, although they do so best in a sunny site. Little pruning needed; thin out some of the older branches each year to encourage strong new fruiting shoots.

RASPBERRIES
Raspberries are somewhat fussy; they do not like soils which are very heavy and slow-draining, very dry in summer, or highly limy (e.g. chalk). Always work plenty of compost or well-rotted manure into the planting site, especially on the types of soil described above. The canes need supporting wires. Summer-fruiting varieties crop on the previous season's canes. After fruiting, cut out the canes which have produced the year's crop, and tie in the current season's new canes to fruit the following year. Autumn-fruiting varieties crop

on the current year's new canes, which should be cut down completely in February.

STRAWBERRIES
If planted in August or September, strawberries will crop the following year. Planted in spring, they will not become established enough to fruit well the same year, but will produce a good crop

Protect strawberries from soil-splashing with straw or cut-out mats.

Protect the strawberry crop from birds with fine netting. Peg netting securely with twigs or cane.

the following summer. Work plenty of compost or rotted manure into the bed. Keep young plants well watered during dry weather to help them settle in; and water as the fruits start to ripen if the weather is dry. Root runners during summer in pots of peat-based compost, to provide plants for new beds, so that you can replace your first strawberry bed when it becomes worn out and stops cropping.

Planting and pruning raspberries: Dig a trench and fill with humus-enriched soil. Plant canes 12-18in. apart with the roots running along the trench.

After planting (in autumn or late winter) prune canes down to 6-9in. As the new canes grow, tie them into wires stretched between posts.

After cropping, prune summer fruiting raspberries by removing the old fruited canes and tying in young ones. Autumn fruiting types should be cut down completely in late winter.

95

PRUNING AND CUTTING BACK

When should you prune?

Pruning is a subject which often worries inexperienced gardeners, and one of the commonest gardening mistakes is to prune at the wrong time of year. But the basic rules are quite straight-forward.

Trees, shrubs and climbers which flower early in the year, in late winter, spring or early summer (up to about the end of June), produce their flowers on the shoots which grew the previous summer. If you need to prune these early-flowering types, it is best done as soon as possible after they finish flowering. This will then ensure that they have as much time as possible after pruning in order to grow new flowering shoots for the following year's display.

Those which flower in late summer and on into autumn (from the end of June onwards) do so on the current year's new shoots. If you need to prune these, do so during a frost-free spell in late winter or early spring (generally late February and March, but be guided by the weather, waiting for a mild spell). This encourages plenty of strong new shoots which will flower the same year.

How often do you need to prune?

Most trees, shrubs and climbers do not need regular pruning. Given enough space to grow and expand, they will continue flowering happily year after year quite naturally. Indeed the slower-growing types will often take some time to recover and start flowering freely again after being cut hard back.

The main reasons for pruning ornamental plants are these : (1) because the plant has grown too large for its allocated space; (2) because it is necessary to improve the appearance of an unsightly mis-shapen plant; (3) because it has stopped flowering freely, having become a congested tangle of worn-out old branches which are reluctant to produce young flowering shoots; (4) because branches or shoots have become diseased or have died, in which case the affected wood should be removed as soon as possible to prevent rot from spreading to healthy wood.

When pruning to reduce the size of a plant or to encourage renewed flowering, try to avoid giving it an all-over trim, which will spoil its natural shape and result in a totally unnatural hedgehog-look (unless, of course you want to trim small-leaved evergreens into fancy topiary shapes). Instead, reach into the shrub and cut the longest and straggliest old branches and shoots hard back, leaving the shorter and younger growths. This will produce a plant which is both neater and less congested (which will encourage new flowering shoots to develop), but which will retain its

natural shape. If you are forced to cut an overgrown shrub right back to stumps (in late winter or early spring) in an attempt to drastically reduce its size, always try to leave some leafy shoots on the stumps to increase the chances of regrowth.

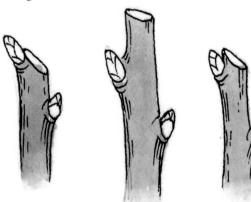

Pruning technique: (a) Incorrect pruning cut; too close to the bud below. (b) Incorrect; too far above the bud. The stub may become diseased and cause die-back of the shoot. (c) Correct.

It should be obvious from the above that annual pruning is not generally essential. It may be necessary after a number of years' growth, or it may never be necessary; all depends on the type and vigour of the plant and whether it was given enough growing room in the first place.

But there are some notable exceptions. Some shrubs are grown mainly for their colourful and attractive new shoots or young leaves (such as the red-stemmed dogwoods, or the silvery-blue leafed eucalyptus). These are usually cut hard back every spring, just before bud-burst, to ensure a good flush of young growths. Some low-growing shrubs, such as heathers and lavender, are commonly trimmed over with shears after flowering to remove dead flower heads and straggly shoots. Do not cut them back into the plants' old wood.

Formal bush roses (the popular 'hybrid tea' and 'floribunda' varieties) are pruned annually to maintain neat growth and good flowering. In the autumn, shorten any particularly tall shoots by about a third to a half, to prevent the bush from being rocked by winter winds. In the spring, remove any dead wood and weak spindly shoots, then cut back all remaining shoots to within a few buds of the base of the previous year's growth. Informal shrub roses need little pruning.

Clematis often foxes gardeners. The simple answer is that the most common species (such as *Clematis montana* and *C. tangutica*) need no regular pruning, unless they spread too far and become a nuisance. Large-flowered hybrid clematis, which flowers early (May to June), does so on

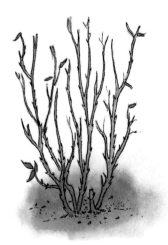

Pruning a Hybrid Tea rose bush: Cut out any dead, diseased or broken shoots, pruning them back to healthy live wood. Also remove any shoots which cross each other and are likely to rub. Prune back the remaining shoots to about 10in. from the ground. Cut back weak thin shoots to encourage stronger regrowth. Prune thick strong stems less severely. Make pruning cuts to just above outward-facing buds to encourage open bushy growth.

the previous year's shoots and should therefore be pruned soon after flowering. Hybrids which bloom in late summer and early autumn flower on the current year's growths; so you can prune them hard back in February and March if you want to keep them tidy.

What can you do about overgrown hedges?

Overgrown hedges are a common problem, but in most cases the solution is quite simple. Deciduous hedges may be cut hard back during a frost-free spell in late winter (late February or March), evergreens should be tackled in early spring (March or early April). Even if cut down to stumps, most hedging plants should eventually produce new growth, especially if fed, and watered in dry weather.

Take care with conifers, however. You can cut down the tops of conifer hedges a little to reduce height. But if you cut hard back into the sides, to reduce thickness, you may create bare brown patches which will be very slow to green up again (or may never do so). Yew is quick to make new growth from bare wood, but the more modern conifer hedging plants can be a real problem and are best treated cautiously.

WEED PROBLEMS

What is the best way to deal with weeds?

There are two types of weed — fast-growing annual weeds, which sprout quickly from seeds every year and are easily hoed-off at the roots, and long-lived perennial weeds (such as nettles, dandelions, docks, bindweed and couch grass), which grow larger and spread into wider clumps from year to year and whose roots must be either dug out or killed with chemicals. You will soon learn to recognize them and tell them apart. Digging and hand-weeding are the traditional methods of clearing weedy ground and, if soil is manageable, to be recommended. If you do the job thoroughly, you can be sure of getting out those deep weed roots which, if left in the ground, will cause increasing problems later.

If the spread of weeds is extensive, you can spray or sprinkle with a 'translocated' weedkiller, which kills weed foliage and is also taken down into the roots of perennial weeds for total kill above and below ground. The latest chemical of this sort is Glyphosate, which kills perennial weeds slowly but surely. Glyphosate does not poison the soil, and planting may take place within a fairly short period after application (check instructions on bottles). Garden shops will advise on available brands. Take care not to splash or spray the weedkiller on to garden plants or crops, as even a slight contact with their leaves can cause serious damage or death to the plants.

What about weeds amongst garden plants and in lawns?

Annual weed seedlings among garden plants and crops should be hoed off as they appear throughout the year. Deep-rooted and stubborn perennial weeds which are growing among garden plants, and are difficult to spray or sprinkle with weedkiller without harming the plants, may be treated with a 'spot' weedkiller. Glyphosate is available in a spot-killer jelly form, specifically for painting on perennial weed leaves in such situations (to kill both leaves and roots). Spot-treatment Glyphosate may similarly be used to treat weeds in lawns without harming the grass.

PESTS, DISEASES AND DISORDERS

Bear in mind that more and more gardeners these days are becoming environmentally conscious and trying to minimize the use of pesticides. Avoid spraying routinely 'as a precaution', which is not only an environmentally questionable practice, but can be wasteful and expensive. Instead, spray when a problem occurs, and then act fast to prevent it from getting out of hand.

How do you identify and deal with pest and disease problems?

Identifying pests, diseases and other plant disorders is not always an easy task for the inexperienced gardener (nor even for an experienced one), since a number of different troubles may produce very similar symptoms. If you experience persistent problems, the cause of which you cannot pinpoint, refer to a comprehensive reference book.

The common problem of damage from slugs and snails is easily recognised and easily remedied by putting down slug pellets (preferably in a bird- and animal-proof slug-trap container, available from some garden shops and mail-order catalogues). The non-chemical alternative is to sink bowls in the soil and fill with beer dregs — slugs like a tipple and will be drawn to the bowls, get drunk, fall in and drown. Or — if you are not squeamish go out with a torch at night (when slugs and snails are active) and collect them for disposal in the dustbin. You will find that many plant pests are particularly active after dark, and a sortie with a torch may unmask that mysterious marauder which has been munching your plants. Minor infestations of greenfly may be dealt with by squashing the pests against the leaf with your thumb. More serious infestations should be given repeated sprays with a malathion insecticide. This chemical will also kill various other leaf-sucking pests. If the trouble persists, try a 'systemic' insecticide, which is absorbed into the plant's foliage and stays there for a prolonged period, being ingested by any insect which nibbles or sucks at the foliage.

The simplest remedy for common fungal diseases (leaf-spots, grey mould, powdery mildews, all of which are fairly obvious when they strike) is a general-purpose systemic fungicide. It may not cure every fungal disease, but it should help with most of the ones you are likely to encounter.

When spraying insecticide, take care to wet the undersides of the leaves as well as the tops as this is where many pests are to be found. Do not spray plants in flower, to avoid killing bees.

Suitable general fungicides include benomal and thiophanate-methyl (garden shops will advise on available brands). These systemic fungicides, like the systemic insecticides, are absorbed by plant foliage for prolonged protection.

Is the problem a pest, a disease, or some other disorder?

The signs of pest attack are usually obvious: infestations of insects on leaves, nibbled or holed foliage, stems chewed off at ground level, or roots eaten away by underground grubs. Closer investigation of the foliage or the soil will usually identify the culprit.

Fungal diseases, too, are usually obvious: yellow, brown or black leaf-spots, fluffy moulds, warty scabs, and white, black or rusty-coloured powdery coatings.

If a plant is unhealthy but there are no signs of pests or disease, then the trouble is most likely to have arisen from the growing conditions. First check the soil. Is it too dry or too wet? Both conditions can cause similar symptoms of wilting foliage and, eventually, browned leaves and die-back. Dry soil causes the obvious drought problems. Waterlogged soil causes roots to rot, so that moisture cannot be taken up by the plant; and the end result is much the same as with a shortage of water. Waterlogged soil and rotting roots indicate a soil-drainage problem.

If dry or waterlogged soil does not appear to be causing the problem, try feeding with a liquid fertilizer, preferably one containing 'trace elements', in case a shortage of plant foods is the cause of the worry. If your soil is limy, check that the plant is not a lime-hater.

The other possibility is damage from the weather. Remember that constant wind on an exposed site will worsen drought problems, increasing the danger of plant leaves scorching and browning. If the garden is very windy, check whether the plant prefers a well-sheltered site, and think about planting hedges or tall shrubs for general wind-shelter. Frost-scorching is the most obvious and frequent form of damage from weather. Like drought problems, it is made worse on an exposed site where freezing easterly winds tear at plants during winter. It also tends to be common in low-lying gardens surrounded by higher ground, where cold air flows down slopes and settles in a 'frost pocket'. Plants which are repeatedly scorched by freezing winter weather should be covered or wrapped with insulating materials (sacking, straw, etc.) during prolonged freezes. Remove these coverings during milder spells to let the plants breathe and to prevent the growth of fungal diseases.

Take care, also, to protect tender or half-hardy bedding plants if frosts are forecast after you have planted them out in late spring. The risk of cold-weather damage to bedding plants should always be minimized by 'hardening off' the plants before they go into the garden soil. 'Hardening off' simply means that you should gradually get the plants used to cooler conditions over a period of a fortnight or more, putting them outside on mild days and taking them back under cover if it turns cold and frosty.

Why won't it flower?

If a shrub or climber refuses to flower properly, you may be pruning it at the wrong time of year. Or it may be growing in the wrong situation. Most plants flower better in sunny sites than in shade, and some must have lots of sun to bloom well. Check the plant's requirements.

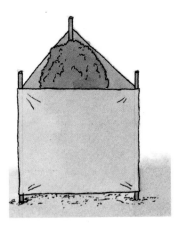

Shrubs and large plants prone to frost damage may be protected during severe winter weather with an all-round screen of polythene sheet or sacking stretched around canes or stakes. Packing with straw or dry bracken will provide added insulation against cold.

On exposed windy sites, young shrubs may grow better if given the shelter of a wind-break such as sacking tied between canes or stakes, on the side facing the prevailing winds. Young evergreen shrubs and conifers in particular suffer in very windy situations.

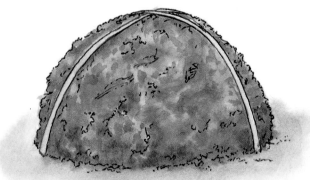

Small shrubs and border plants which suffer winter frost damage may be protected with a layer of straw or dried bracken held down with netting pegged into the soil, or with twigs or canes.

Too much nitrogen fertilizer or manure may induce excessive leafy growth at the expense of flowering. Or, if the plant is a new one recently planted, then it may simply be putting its energies into growing roots and shoots before flowering. In either case, feeding with a high-potash, liquid fertilizer (e.g. tomato fertilizer) or with sulphate of potash should encourage free-flowering.

99

PROPAGATION PLANTS

How can you raise your own plants?

The most common methods of plant propagation are from seed, from cuttings and by division. All types of plant may be grown from seed, but trees, shrubs, climbers and some bulbs take many years to reach flowering size when raised this way; it is fun to try, but you need lots of patience. Bear in mind, also, that seeds from a named variety will produce a plant somewhat different in flower and other characteristics from the parent plant. If you want to produce plants identical to the parent in every way, you must propagate 'vegetatively', by cuttings or division.

Annuals for summer bedding must be raised from seed. Perennial border plants may be raised from seed, from cuttings or by division, depending on the type. Bulbs are increased by dividing the clumps when the leaves die down. Trees, shrubs and climbers are propagated from cuttings.

Many clump-forming perennial border plants may be increased by division in the autumn or spring.

After lifting separate the larger plants by prising clump apart with two garden forks back-to-back.

Take 8-12in. long hardwood shrub cuttings in late autumn.

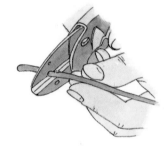

Cut off the soft tip above a bud and trim base just below a bud.

Plant out the divisions as quickly as possible, firm into the soil and water thoroughly.

Smaller plants may be divided by teasing the clumps apart with your fingers.

Sprinkle sharp sand into a narrow slit-trench and insert cuttings.

In summer, root smaller semi-hard shoots in a propagator or frame.

Most propagation problems arise from not checking the exact requirements of individual plants. Some seeds (such as those of half-hardy annuals) need artificial heat to germinate well; but they need only a little, as too high a temperature can prevent sprouting just as much as one too low. Other seeds (those of hardy perennials, hardy bulbs, alpines, shrubs, trees and climbers) will often germinate better if given cool or cold treatment for a period. The correct time to take cuttings also varies from one plant to another. Always check individual requirements in seed catalogues and gardening encyclopaedias.

The next most common mistake is the failure to use a proper seed compost and clean pots and trays for sowing. Buying good-quality seed compost is essential. Garden soil will not do, as it may be full of weed seeds and disease spores. Always ensure that sowing containers are thoroughly clean. Fungal diseases linger in traces of old soil or compost in dirty pots and trays and can quickly wipe out your seedlings. If seedlings do start to die off, water with Cheshunt Compound (available from garden shops). Always sow seed thinly. Over-thick sowing is another common mistake, and one which inevitably results in crowded, spindly seedlings which are apt to rot.

On semi-hard cuttings, trim off all but the top 4-5 leaves.

100 *Sow seed thinly for best results.*

GARDENING CALENDAR

SPRING

● From late winter to early spring, sow half-hardy annuals in warmth; alternatively, buy ready-grown plants in late spring. Hardy annuals may be sown later, in trays or directly into prepared beds and borders. Sow hardy perennial seeds in a cold frame or an unheated glasshouse.

● Start sowing vegetable seeds when the soil has dried out and warmed up enough. Most should be sown in the beds where they are to grow, but others need to be started in seed beds and transplanted later, and a few should be started under glass (check requirements). Start planting seed potatoes when the worst of the frosts are over.

● Take cuttings of herbaceous border plants and tender perennials as they sprout new growth.

● Give established plants a top-dressing of balanced compound fertilizer to boost growth.

● Plant border perennials, shrubs, trees, climbers and summer-flowering bulbs. Herbaceous border plants which have made wide clumps may be lifted and divided.

● Prune 'hybrid tea' and 'floribunda' bush roses.

● Spring is a good time to sow or turf new lawns. Seed over bare patches on existing lawns. First do any soil-improvement that may be necessary.

SUMMER

● Watering, weeding, lawn-mowing and hedge-clipping are the all-too-obvious main tasks in this season. Do not forget to feed lawns.

● Half-hardy annuals and tender bedding perennials may be planted out in late spring or early summer, once the danger of late frosts is past. Make sure they have been 'hardened off' (gradually acclimatized to outdoor conditions).

● Take semi-hard cuttings of the current year's shoots from trees, shrubs and climbers. Root strawberry runners into pots of compost, to provide extra plants for a new bed.

● Continue to sow salad vegetables for season-long crops. Keep well watered in dry weather.

● Protect soft fruit from birds. After summer-fruiting raspberries have been cropped, cut down all the cane which bore fruit and tie-in young canes of the present year's growth.

● In late summer (August) buy and plant autumn-flowering bulbs.

AUTUMN

● Plant perennial border plants, shrubs, trees, climbers and spring-flowering bulbs.

● Give established permanent plants a second dose of compound fertilizer in early autumn.

● Take hardwood cuttings of trees, shrubs and climbers.

● Dig up tender bedding perennials and tender bulbs, to be kept frost-free over winter.

● On clay soils, rough-dig empty ground as early as possible, to encourage frost-action to break it down.

WINTER

● Fork manure into empty vegetable garden areas.

● Cover empty vegetable beds with polythene sheets, to encourage early drying and warming in spring and so make early sowings possible.

● If any of your plants are prone to frost-damage, protect them during prolonged severe freezes, with straw, sacking, etc.

● In February, cut autumn-fruiting raspberries down to the ground.

101

INDEX